A PIECE OF PIE

EVERYDAY MIRACLES SERVED EVERY DAY

Dan Cassidy and many others

A PIECE OF PIE

EVERYDAY MIRACLES SERVED EVERY DAY

*A*dvantage
BOOKS

By Dan Cassidy and many others

Dan Cassidy and many others

A Piece of Pie by Daniel Cassidy
ISBN: 978-1-59755-508-1

Published by: ADVANTAGE BOOKS™
                  Longwood, Florida, USA
                  www.advbookstore.com

   Bible quotations are from THE HOLY BIBLE, NEW INTERNATIONAL VERSION®, NIV® Copyright © 1973, 1978, 1984, 2011 by Biblica, Inc.® Used by permission. All rights reserved worldwide. The "NIV" and "New International Version" are trademarks registered in the United States Patent and Trademark Office by Biblica Inc
MOMENTS OF LOVE Reprinted with permission of Loyola Press from the book *The Power of Miracles*, By Joan Webster Anderson copyright 1998,2005

Library of Congress Catalog Number: 2019946170
1.   Religion: Christian Life - Inspirational

First Printing: August 2019
19 20 21 22 23 24 25   10 9 8 7 6 5 4 3 2 1
Printed in the United States of America

DEDICATION

This book is dedicated to God. It was He that performed the miracles in this book. None but the Highest God could do these things. So, in the words of King Nebuchadnezzar:

> *"To the peoples, nations and men of every language, who live in all the world: May you prosper greatly! It is my pleasure to tell you about the miraculous signs and wonders the Most High God has performed for me."* ***Daniel 4:1***

He has healed many, delivered many from their sins and addictions, prevented accidents saved lives, and given us blessings both small and large. He has also told us that time is short, and what we should do with the time we have been given. The Lord has done all these great works, including bringing many testimonies to us, in order to strengthen our faith and to bring His truth to those who still walk in darkness.

This book is also dedicated to the men and women who have given of their time, talents, and hearts to give their testimonies to us. Also, to my wife Sharon, and friend Dean Wagers, whose contributions made the bookmarks and this book possible.

My heartfelt thanks go out to Noel McDonnell and Dr. Damien Dupuis whose suggestions and revisions have improved the book significantly. And to my sister Pam and her husband Dave, the two people who have been there for me, in my darkest days. I will forever be in their debt.

To God alone goes the glory!

ABOUT THE AUTHORS

The authors are single, married, young and old, rich and poor. They come from all walks of life; construction workers, teachers, students, pastors, office workers and those retired from all walks of life. People just like you, people not special or saints, people who like you – loved by our Lord, who loves all people and constantly reaches out to them.

The collector of these testimonies, Dan Cassidy, is a retired factory and construction worker and a sinner. The Lord has graciously given him some of the testimonies and has given him the added blessing of collecting these testimonies from others. They were given by friends and strangers; some gave us their stories before they gave us their names.

Whenever the testimonies were given in a written way, they appear in their own words. If the testimonies were given orally, the transcriptions were created as accurately as possible. Minor corrections have been made for spelling, syntax, grammar, punctuation and narrative clarity where appropriate. Some names have been changed to protect the blessed.

Dan's notation:

I thank God. He has blessed me by permitting me to hear these many testimonies first-hand. Shortly after a men's retreat in 2014 in which The Holy Spirit gave me the message that "Time is short.", people started sharing their testimonies with me. The Lord put it on my heart to compile this book. These testimonies have made my faith stronger; I pray they do the same for you. While hearing these testimonies, I have experienced a strong spiritual connection with my brothers and sisters in Christ. There has been joy and sometimes tears. So overpowering is His love, it can be overwhelming. I am sure that you can experience it too. All you need to do is share your testimony with others.

When I first started to compile the testimonies, I planned on writing them in the order I received them, with testimonies simply numbered one to an unknown number. This would make it easier for a poor writer, speller and typist. He could have chosen anyone of His talented writers to do this book, however, to show His power and His sense of humor, He chose me. Sorry for your luck. Fortunately for all, many of the co-authors are very good writers. I later realized they should be in chapters based on of type of experience, though many testimonies could fit in many chapters, as they transcend a single experience or definition. Each testimony individually shows us something of the nature of God. Taken together, even more is revealed. The comments placed at the beginning or end of some testimonies are what He revealed to me. He may have a different revelation for you.

If you have not yet decided your faith, have doubts or questions; I strongly encourage you to keep reading with an open mind and heart. Within these testimonies you may find your answers.

Notes from the photographer:

Table Mountain Church (TMC) is not affiliated with the author of this book. TMC serves as a place of worship, and a communal gathering place. The building which houses TMC has a remarkable history; it was first the town high school (completed in 1922) and a gymnasium was added in 1938. In 2011, TMC purchased the property. For over 96 years, in one form or another, the building itself has served the local community as a place of common assembly, but most of all, it has served as a place to learn and grow. Whether in the form of athletics, academics or in the dedication to life-long growth in the Holy Spirit, individuals have received many lessons from within the walls of TMC. The photographer wishes to express her thanks to TMC for the generous use of their communal space at no cost, and for all the things learned while the photography shoot was in session.

Pie Hand Model: Nick Chucka

I would like to hand it to Nick for his dutiful repose during the photography session. He held his arm in one spot longer than reasonable, *without complaint*, and with gratitude.

"But the Lord stood at my side and gave me strength." **2 Timothy 4:17**

A Recipe Testimony Substitution, by Noel McDonnell

For every testimony included in this book, there are others which transpired in various locations; in diners and parks, in churches and clubhouses, in nature and in cityscapes, in houses and hot tubs, and each one of them is unique to their own moment in time. It's a metaphorical still-shot for those who were paying attention. There were those who were present and bore witness to stories spoken from the heart, but never transcribed. There were eyes and ears open to receiving the truth of words explaining one's experience or connection to God, Jesus Christ, or the Holy Spirit. It's through these collective exposures, both magnificent and minuscule, which spur individuals to achieve purpose in living their values and using their God-given talents for good. While their stories may not be documented in the physicality, they remain etched in a sketch in the memories of those who were in proximity.

These are precious moments which hold sentiment and influence others to varying degrees. It is the personal interactions and polarity of our everyday choices which make the deepest impacts in our world. So, as we go about our days, making the most of the time we are given with the ingredients we have, keep in mind the stories we are writing with everyone we meet and greet along the way, regardless if it is written down.

TABLE OF CONTENTS

DEDICATION 5

ABOUT THE AUTHORS...6

SECTION ONE: TESTIMONIES

CHAPTER ONE: MEETINGS WITH SPIRITUAL BEINGS.........................15

ANGEL ON A PARK BENCH 15

GOD ATTENDS A FUNERAL 16

ANGELS AND DEMONS..17

PLEASE MOM STOP PRAYING 18

GOD GOES TO CHURCH 19

ROOF TOP DANCER 20

VISITATION OF ANGELS..21

ANGEL AT A CONCERT 25

MY ENCOUNTER WITH GOD..27

ANOTHER ENCOUNTER WITH GOD 29

CHAPTER TWO: REDEMPTION AND DELIVERANCE.............................31

TESTIMONY OF A FOURTEEN-YEAR-OLD....................................31

DRUG ADDICT FOUND 32

A VETERANS TESTIMONY 32

PASTOR MARK OTTEN..35

REBIRTH..38

A BLIND MAN HELPS ME SEE 40

A STORY OF FAITH, HOPE, AND LOVE 43

SUZY'S STORY...48

DYSFUNCTIONAL FAMILY TO GOD'S FAMILY 50

CHAPTER THREE: HEALING 57

    HEALING TESTIMONY 57

    THE LORD HAS HEALED ME 57

    HEAD INJURY 58

    YES YOU 59

    YEAH GOD! 59

    OUT OF THE ICU... 60

    DAN'S NOTATION: 61

CHAPTER FOUR: PHYSICAL LIVES SAVED 63

    ON THE OTHER SIDE 63

    THE CATCH 64

    THE LADY WITH THE ROSARY TATOO 65

    GOD'S SUPERNATURAL INTERVENTION 66

    PROTECTING BUBBLE.. 67

    EACH DAY IS A GIFT 68

    ROCKY'S ROAD 72

    THE ANGEL'S PROTECTION 72

    OVER TURNED TRUCK... 73

    PEDAL TO THE METAL.. 74

    HAND OF GOD 75

CHAPTER FIVE: RETURNED FROM THE OTHER SIDE 77

    ADDICT SENT BACK 77

    A FOGGY MORNING... 77

    SPEAKING TO JESUS 78

    IN THE FOOTSTEPS OF ELIJAH 78

    GOD ANSWERS PRAYER... 79

CHAPTER SIX: OTHER BLESSINGS 81

    WHO NEEDS THE MAYTAG REPAIRMAN?..................... 81

    HELPING HAND PLUMBING 81

    WHICH WAY DO I GO? 82

    A PIECE OF PIE.. 83

    A SPECIAL BLESSING FOR ME 83

    BAPTISM.. 84

FORGIVENESS 85
IDOL BURNING MOM 85
MIRACLE GIRL 85
GIFT OF A ROSARY 86
SOMETHING CRAZY 87
ANNE'S YEARS OF SERVICE TO THE LORD 88
TO EVERLASTING RICHES - CAPTAIN OF MY SHIP 89
HOME EARLY 91
TESTIMONIES FROM JERUSALEM 91
MEETING A PROPHET 93
TRIP TO ORLANDO 95
A PRIVATE JOKE 97
IT IS GOING TO BE A RAINY DAY 98

SECTION TWO: TIME IS SHORT AND WHAT MAY BE

CHAPTER SEVEN: TIME IS SHORT; THE MESSAGE 103
RETREAT TESTIMONY 105
BOOKMARK EXPLAINED 106
HOW THE PASSAGES WERE CHOSEN 112

CHAPTER EIGHT: DREAMS 115
CHIP TESTIMONY FROM WYOMING 115
WILD DOGS 116
MARK OF THE BEAST 117
NEW TEMPLE 118
WHAT WAS OURS 119

CHAPTER NINE: PROPHECIES OF HIS RETURN 123
PROPHECIES OF HIS RETURN 123
WHAT IT ALL MEANS TO ME 126
ANOTHER ANGEL ENCOUNTER 128
THE BEGINNING 131

RECOMMENDED READING 132

GLOSSARY 133

Dan Cassidy and many others

Section One

Testimonies

Dan Cassidy and many others

Chapter One

Meetings With Spiritual Beings

Since ancient times, God has sent His angels, and has sometimes appeared Himself to His children, for His own purpose. As He has done, so He continues to do.

In the sixth month of Elizabeth pregnancy, God sent the angel Gabriel to Nazareth, a town in Galilee. **Luke 1:26**

ANGEL ON A PARK BENCH

I, Dan E., had dropped out of college in spring because of financial issues combined with my sudden realization that I was in the wrong major. That realization had come about after much prayer and a month of real soul searching at college.

During the following summer, I worked at a Christian camp; one where I had become a Christian about six years previous. The camp had promised me full-time employment after summer ended, but they reneged on the offer two weeks before I was to start as full-time. This change affected permanent staff because they changed their policy so that all full-timers were required to have a college degree. I was crushed. I'd already moved everything I owned up to the camp. Now I had to go back to my parents' place with my tail between my legs.

A pastor friend, Terry, knew I was struggling with what to do next and offered to take me to lunch to talk it out. He worked at College Hill Presbyterian Church in Cincinnati.

The church has a courtyard area with a concrete bench that surrounds a large tree. To get to the courtyard, you can walk down three narrow walkways that are bordered by buildings. The only other way in is on the east side, where one of the buildings empties into the courtyard.

Terry was going to be a few minutes, so I waited under the tree.

After a few minutes, an elderly woman with a cane came walking down the walkway from the parking lot. She took her time getting to the bench and sat down on my left. She wore an old-fashioned dress peach in color, with a white lace collar. She had the most vibrant smile. Before I could even say hi, she spoke.

"Dan" she said in a sweet, kindly voice, *"I've been talking to the Lord about you. He says you should pursue helping others in whatever setting you like most"* She said it with so much, conviction that I began to tear up.

While I was trying to choke back tears and process how it was that this stranger knew my name – because I had never seen her before in my life – Terry came out of the building on my right.

I waved, then immediately turned back to the woman, who had utterly vanished.

Terry came up. *"You looked like you were talking to someone."*

"Didn't you see the old lady who was talking to me?"

"There wasn't anyone that I saw," he said.

"Terry. She was sitting on my left. She was right there!!! Terry. She was sitting on my left. She was right there!"

"Dan, I didn't see anyone."

Wow.

Here's the thing: I've always paid special heed to elderly Christian women. If God was going to send me a message, that would be the perfect messenger.

Terry and I had a lot to talk about over lunch.

GOD ATTENDS A FUNERAL

In late 2014, while shopping in a Big-box home improvement store, I passed by a young mother with her infant. I overheard her telling one of the store clerks that her baby had been diagnosed with a serious food allergy. I asked the mother for her permission to pray for her baby. She said yes, so I prayed for her child.

When I finished, I told her to have the baby retested, and she thanked me for the prayer. We talked a while longer about her baby and also my grandniece, who has a severe peanut allergy. Then we talked about our faith and the Lord.

She informed me that she is a Catholic. I told her I have a Catholic background, though I currently attend a nondenominational church.

Then as much to my surprise as hers I said, *"You have seen God!"* She replied, *"Not to my knowledge."* I told her to think back over her life and she would recall seeing someone; someone who when your eyes met, you had a feeling of wellbeing and of peace that was over whelming.

Her response was immediate *"At my grandfather's funeral!"*

Dan's notation:

These two testimonies show some the love and concern of our Father. The young woman was given the feeling of peace and joy that can only be experienced in the presence of God during a time of sorrow and mourning. Our God is caring and compassionate to us all.

ANGELS AND DEMONS

Early one morning I was sitting on the porch of a log cabin in the Ozarks. A man was passing by and he and I exchanged greetings. He continued on his way. After he had traveled some forty feet or so, he turned and came back.

He proceeded to tell me about his father's passing. His father was in a hospital room dying, surrounded by his family. He became very agitated watching something outside his window.

He then cried out *"Don't you see them? Don't you see them?"* Over and over he asked. His family responded that they saw nothing. He said, *"There are angels and demons fighting over my soul!"* This continued for several minutes. He became calm and again asked, *"Don't you see them?"* repeatedly.

Once more, his family responded that they saw nothing. With a smile on his face, his father said, *"Mary, Joseph and the baby are standing beside my bed."* The man's father died shortly after that.

But even the archangel Michael, when he was disputing with the devil about the body of Moses, did not dare to bring a slanderous accusation against him, but said "The Lord rebuke you" **Jude 1:9**

Dan's notation:

This testimony is about a man who must have known of Jesus but had not ever turned his life over to Him completely. On the edge of the cliff, Satan thought he could lay claim to his soul. Thank God that Jesus is the Good Shepherd who will reach for His sheep even as they fall off the cliff. He will be there for each of us, both believer and unbeliever alike, to welcome us home, or to give one last chance to come to Him.

This testimony gives us hope for all that have died. Loved ones that we believe were not saved; for the atheist, or the members of non-Christian churches. The Good Shepherd was there for this man and many may have turned to Him even in the last microsecond of their lives. Our God is indeed the God who saves.

PLEASE MOM STOP PRAYING

This testimony has been given to us in White Sulphur Spring, Montana, by a man whose actions say, "This is a Christian." The testimony is not about him, however. It concerns a neighbor and friend of his son.

His son's friend was a very young, frail boy. He suffered from an auto-immune disease like "The disease the boy in the 'glass bubble' movie suffered from." The boy was not placed in a bubble even though he was at a very high risk for infection. Not wanting their son to live in isolation, the boy's parents used a different approach in caring for their son. They did their best to keep him from contracting diseases. They used medicines such as antibiotics. They kept him away from places and people where he could become infected, without totally isolating him.

He made a friend; the two boys were neighbors. The man's son was a big boy, but with a very gentle personality. That is why the sick boy's parents allowed them to play together.

Despite their best efforts and prayers, the boy became ill. As he grew weaker and weaker to the point of death, his mother prayed for his recovery. Until one day; while she was praying, her son said to her *"Please stop praying; Jesus is standing here waiting for me."*

Dan's notation:

A mother praying for the life of her son. A son blessed, far greater now with Jesus. Thank God for prayers not answered in the way we ask. This testimony shows how our Lord honors our prayers, that before He would let the boy come with Him, his mother had to stop praying for him to stay. He answered her prayers for life until He told her it was time to change her prayer.

GOD GOES TO CHURCH

This is one of the many undeserved blessings that God has given to me, Dan Cassidy, the collector of these testimonies. He has blessed me many times, in so many supernatural ways.

Some fourteen years into my first marriage, I started viewing porn. A little at first, I thought what could it hurt? Then I viewed more and more. Soon, that was not enough for me and I started picking up women; single, married or professional, I didn't care.

My first wife was and is a wonderful person and did not in any way deserve the pain I caused her, for which I am extremely sorry.

In the last weeks of my secret life, I had lost my job. Then my wife confronted me, and I admitted my guilt. There I was, right where my sins had led me. Jobless, homeless and hopeless. Where I belonged. I was reaping that which I had sown. The wages of sin are death. I had certainly killed the life I had known and hurt those who loved me the most.

I went out and purchased a handgun, and I put in it my truck. I planned on using it Sunday night. That Sunday morning, I went to mass at Holy Redeemer Church in Portsmouth, Ohio. I do not know why after not going to church or having Christ in my life for years that I then turned to Him. What I prayed for I do not recall. What I received was His love and mercy.

During the service, a man came down the aisle and I could not take my eyes from him. He was the most distinguished man I had ever seen; His bearing and dress all said this man is a king. I have seen men dressed in suits costing thousands of dollars, but compared to him, they were wearing rags.

I could not stop looking at him. When he reached the pew right in front of the one I was standing in, less than thirty feet away, as our eyes met, I had an over whelming feeling. The feeling was indescribable; of peace, well-being, joy and love that reached right down to my core. This feeling lasted only a few moments. I remember thinking that even if the ceiling was to come crashing down on me at that moment everything would be alright.

I looked up at the ceiling for a moment. When I looked for him, he was no longer visible. I was sitting in a large church, just a little over half way to the back, with many pews behind me. The rear exits were seventy feet away. I turned to check the aisles and every pew behind me. He was not to be seen.

Later that day, I told my brothers about my plan but did not tell them what happened in the church. They removed the gun from my truck. In fact, I never told anyone what occurred in the church that day, until many years later. I would tell them that God had sent one of His angels to save me. This is what I believed had occurred until one night, about ten years ago, while thanking God for His angel, I heard God say, *"That was no angel, that was Me!"*

No wonder He had the bearing of a king. He is the Lord of Lords and the King of Kings.

Many years later He had me meet one of His prophets. Upon meeting this man, he touched me, on my right side, with only one finger, for only a split second. He said, *"You have seen God."*

I would be remiss if I didn't tell you that in God's eyes, I saw only love, compassion and mercy, even though you know some of what I had been doing and what I deserved. Our God is truly a loving and merciful God.

ROOF TOP DANCER

On an evening walk on the Mount of Olives with several others from our hostel, two of us were following a little behind the group. We were a little older and were engrossed in our conversation. The woman I was with told me a few years earlier she had been in the old city of Jerusalem. She told me this:

A joyful procession passed by her, a wedding feast perhaps. The people were laughing, dancing, singing, just having a great time; so much so that she joined them. They went a short distance. She looked up. There on the roof top was our Lord, dressed in a white flowing robe, dancing. As the procession continued, she saw Him once more dancing on the roof's tops of His beloved city.

I thought how blessed the two of us were: to be standing on the Mount of Olives sharing our testimonies of seeing God while still living.

*So Jacob called the place Peniel, saying, "It is because I saw God face to face, and yet my life was spared." **Genesis32:30***

VISITATION OF ANGELS

Account of Pastor Marty Younger

In the next few paragraphs, I am going to share an account of events our congregation experienced in a service about two years ago. It was nothing we were seeking for, and yet we have a hunger for the presence of God in our services each time we have a service. God has blessed us in so many ways, and I do not share this to brag about, or to put down any other service. This just happened by grace and mercy of a loving Father. We began this service like many before and yet there seemed to be a special sense of God's presence in the church. People seemed to be open to a movement of God, and we began worshipping with a deeper zealousness than previously. I remember the presence of God seemed to be getting stronger and stronger as we continued to worship Him. Many began to weep in His presence.

Then, suddenly, I saw an angel come through the ceiling of the church, followed by many more behind him. He stood out as a commander of the rest of the angels, because of his clothing. He had gold bands around each wrist, and seemed to have an armor-like clothing on, very similar to a Roman soldier's uniform. He had long golden hair, but I did not notice any wings.

I mentioned to the congregation that there were angels present, and to my surprise many of the congregation saw them also. One of the youths mentioned that he saw one in the corner of the auditorium which had wings that went out the back of the church and continued outside the building. Others testified that although they did not see them, they knew they were there because some even felt them as they passed by.

What happened next was something that taught our church and me a very valuable lesson. I had always wondered what I would say to an angel if I ever met one. I don't think it can be something you pre-plan. When you are in that presence, it is amazing what goes through your mind. I asked the one I thought the captain of the rest, *"Why have you come?"* He replied, *"We have come to worship God with you."* Needless to say, I was puzzled. I said to myself, Lord I need scripture to back that up. No sooner had I said that, when immediately, Hebrews 1 came to me. *"And again, when God brings His firstborn into the world he says "let all God's angels worship him."* I remember the entire church was on their faces all over the auditorium, weeping and worshipping God. It was awesome.

I had never experienced a service like that before. What happened next was the valuable lesson we learned. I have some very good ushers that are always ready to assist in any way they can. Everyone was prostrated on their faces except for one usher who was trying to get handkerchiefs to all the people weeping.

Needless to say, that was impossible. Soon, I noticed the Captain angel rose up and started to go up through the ceiling, with all the other angels following him. I looked up and said, "No, wait, don't leave." He said, "we have to, but we will be back." About that time the presence of God lifted, and people began to stand up, wondering what was going on.

I remember feeling so grieved in my spirit. I asked the Lord what had happened, and He said that we had grieved His presence. I knew exactly what he meant because of the usher, (although innocently) was interrupting people as they were worshipping the Lord. He should have been worshipping God also and not worrying about the handkerchiefs. We learned that evening that there are times when you do not need to carry out your job or wishes, but must give all your attention to the Lord.

That was the first time the Angels visited in such a powerful way, which will lead up to our next experience with angels. Remember, they did say they would be back!

Many months went by before we had another encounter with the angels. The next one, again, we were not seeking for, but we knew that if it ever happened again, we would shut down our schedule and let God have His.

It was another Sunday evening service, and my son, Jason, was playing the drums that evening for Praise and Worship. He was going through the struggles that many teenagers face with the dealings of God. Choosing the right friends, trying to be "macho," I will just say trying to *adjust to his own manhood.* I remember it being a critical time of his life because of some of the friends he chose were not serving God like we felt they should. (I hope I wasn't too picky). Anyway, I noticed two young men from California had walked into the service and I also knew they were into devil worship. The one boy had been in our church at an earlier age but moved to California to live with his dad who was not a Christian, and as a result, he lost his way. To make a long story short, he was kicked out of his dad's home, so he returned to live with his mom and step-dad, who were members of our church. The terms were, to live there, they had to go to church.

This young man knew my son and went back and sat right where Jason's books were, where Jason would soon be going back there to sit. I was on the platform and I said to myself, *"Lord, I don't want Jason to go sit there."*

Those words barely left my mouth and I heard God speak to me very clear; "He won't" and immediately an angel (I am sure it was that *captain angel* because he was dressed the same as I remembered) came through the ceiling and stood right in front of Jason with his arms on each side of his waist. It was just like if you stationed a guard in front of Jason's drum set. What happened next was indeed a miracle. Jason, through the entire service – which was about two and a half hours in length – never left his drum set. That had never before happened.

Then, one of the praise and worship teams on the platform heard the sound of a mighty army surrounding our church. (He shared this with us later in the service.) I was seeing in the spirit and I saw as from a bird's eye view, our service with angels all around our auditorium in formation. It was like seeing a football stadium from the air at night with the lights all around it. There seemed to be a whole heavenly host of angels in that service. We once again did nothing but stand or kneel in his presence. We knew better this time than to move. For almost an hour, there was total silence in our church. No talking, no crying babies, no clearing throats or coughing. The church is located next to a very busy highway and you could not even hear any sounds of traffic. We are also located close to the airport and there was no sound of airplanes flying over, which always happens in every service. It was awesome to say the least. As we waited in that same presence as before, we then experienced what would have happened if we had not grieved the Holy Spirit the last time.

One of our praise team members by the name of Mark saw Jesus walk into our service that evening! He came through the side door and came down to the front and sat down in one of the chairs in the front row. Although I did not see him with my natural eye, from the awesome presence in that service, I knew he was there. He crossed his legs and put his arms on each chair beside him and began to look around! Others sensed a very powerful presence from heaven. Nobody moved or said anything. Following this, Jesus stood up. I do not know how to explain it, but I knew what he was getting ready to do. With tears in my eyes I said *"Jesus is here to heal you."* He went to many of the people that had infirmities and reached out and touched them. Everyone he touched was healed! The people said that they felt a hand touch them and they were healed! This went on for several minutes.

Toward the end of the total silence, the two young men that were into devil worship had gotten up and left the auditorium. We were told later by another young man that he heard them talking in the hall saying, *"I don't care if I have to sleep under a bridge, I am not going back to that church."* About the time Jesus was finished, one of our female Praise and Worship team on the platform, Flossie Smith, began to do the most beautiful dance while giving a message in tongues. When she finished, she gave the interpretation with the actions of the dance, and it was a beautiful song, to the Lord. It was only then that the angel that was guarding Jason looked over at me and departed through the ceiling again. And it was only then that my son was able to leave his drum set. After the service came to an end, many people testified and confirmed the various manifestations we had experienced in that service. I realize that this has become rather lengthy, but it is very hard to put on paper the awesome presence of the Lord that he chose to share with us that night. What we learned from these services is, many people get tripped up at the presence of angels and start seeking angels instead of Jesus. We did not ask for this and were not seeking it: it just happened. I do know this: that if you will respect angels, and yet keep your attention and worship on Jesus, he will be the next manifestation in your midst.

The sad thing is, many of God's people get caught up in just the VISITATION OF ANGELS!

In conclusion, I would just like to say that I have tried to give as accurate an account of this as I am able. I know it is hard to believe, and I have not tried to make it bigger than it is. One thing I know for sure, if you could magnify this experience ten times beyond what I have put on paper, it would be more accurate to what I felt during those evenings in the presence of angels.

All the angels were standing round the throne and around the elders and the four living creatures. They fell down on their faces before the throne and worshipped God. **Revelation 7:11**

ANGEL AT A CONCERT

Several weeks before the 2015 Clear Mountain Community Church men's retreat, I found myself thinking about Marietta, Ohio. A small river town in the Southeastern Appalachian part of Ohio, near West Virginia.

Decades before, I had worked in Marietta on a construction project for a few weeks. That job kept coming back to mind. Then, I would hear or see this town name over and over. After the 2014 retreat, when the Lord wanted me to be in a certain place and time and wanted me to know, He would send me this pattern.

Since this retreat was to be held close to Marietta, I asked the Lord if He would give me a sign if I should go there. The sign was to hear someone say at the retreat to take a boat out on the Ohio River. On the last night of the retreat one of the men said, *"Take a boat out on the river at Cincinnati."* So, I excused myself and left for Marietta.

When I arrived at the Marietta sign, there was a man named Jason hitchhiking in the rain. I knew he was the reason for my trip. Jason, I would soon learn, is what I would call a *hitch- hiking evangelist.* God calls us all to serve in different ways. The enemy had been giving him a hard time of late. A couple of days before, while he was sleeping, someone stole his pack with what little food and money he had. So, we went and ate some seafood together. I was hungry as well.

Having eaten, I decided to take Jason to a better spot to catch a ride. There is very limited traffic in this area in the middle of the night. He was on his way to Maine to check on his mother. It was October and winter would soon arrive.

On our drive, he blessed me by telling me of an encounter he had at a concert. He was on a field surrounded by a multitude of people, when he saw a beautiful girl walking across the field. To his surprise, she walked right up to him and said, *"You need to Know that JESUS CHRIST WILL BE RETURNING VERY SOON."* She then turned and walked away. She either disappeared into the multitude, or just disappeared.

It is my belief that she was sent to Jason, just as Jason and I were brought together, as a second testimony that *TIME IS SHORT* (a message from the Spirit of God that I was given during the 2014 men's retreat of Clear Mountain Community Church) and that *JESUS OUR KING WILL BE RETURNING VERY SOON!*

Many months later, Sharon and I arrived at a campground in Maine, to work for a few months. In our first days there, we met Robert, a fellow camper who was also working for the campground. While sitting at his campfire, I told him about my encounter with Jason and his testimony. Robert then told me that Jason is a good friend of his. Later he gave me Jason's email address. I have written Jason to ask if he would send me his account of his meeting with the angel and with me for this book. If it is not included, that is because he never sent it.

Before arriving in Maine, I only knew one other Mainer, which was Jason. The odds, of meeting someone who knew him? A million to one? No; one to one. God ordained it. He directed us all to show us His power.

MY ENCOUNTER WITH GOD

We were so excited because we had a camping trip planned. It rained, so we went to the Olive Garden for lunch, then a movie. The movie appeared black and white to me and so did everything outside. My husband knew something was wrong. The retina specialist I had been seeing for three years had sent a stat referral to a neurologist on August 9th – this was August 11th – and no one had called on the referral. We went to the neurologist at 5 PM. For some reason, he didn't leave early, or even on time.

Hello, God – You worked that out.

He took one look at my MRI, said I needed a neurosurgeon immediately, and sent me downstairs where they were waiting for us. The neurosurgeon had just finished a surgery and came back into his office. Thank you, God; you kept him in the hospital. He looked at my MRI and said he was admitting me, doing another MRI, and that he would do surgery at 7 AM on Friday, August 12th, and it would take seven and a half hours.

I came out of surgery and knew everyone around me – a miracle. I could feed myself peas with a fork and not drop one, God is so good. Ten days later, I had a setback, and I was in surgery again for three hours. I was in the hospital from August 11th to August 25th.

One night, I was in my bed. It was quiet except for the normal hospital noises. My husband was asleep in the recliner – I felt a presence beside my bed and looked to see who it was. There was no clear picture of a person. I held my hand up and felt someone take it. Then, I knew it was God. I asked if He had come to take me home. The reply was *"No, not now, but I will be with you every step of the way and I will heal you in My time."*

Dan's notation:

About one year after collecting this testimony, I received the following email:

Hello there. I was so excited when I saw your e-mail. I think you were going to Colorado for the birth of a grandchild the last time we saw you.

We are at our home in Florida. We will be going camping in Louisiana at the end of the week but will only be there for a week.

The Lord has not chosen to heal my eye yet. I have shared my testimony so many times and pray that He will continue to use me. I did see the ophthalmologists last week and he said that he believes there is enough movement in the eye to warrant talking to a specialist in the field. I will see him on June 4th and will keep you posted. I have been doing GREAT and give GOD THE GLORY. I drive a lot now and have even driven our motorhome. Progress is evident.

I will let you know what is happening and look forward to hearing from you... even meeting up with you sometime.

God bless.

Dan's notation:

This is the follow up email after the visit to the eye specialist:

Hi there! It was so nice to get your message. My appointment with the specialist went well. I was really nervous and cried on the way to his office. While we were waiting in the exam room, I was praying, and so was my husband. We were holding hands but sending up our own prayers, knowing that the other was praying also. Suddenly, I felt a warm feeling all over and immediately felt a calmness that a nonbeliever would not understand.

The doctor came in, and after talking about how my eye got this way, he had me do some exercises to check the movement. Final decision: I would not benefit from opening the eye. It would only cause confusion in what I was seeing. He said to keep that eye in reserve because if something should happen to my good eye, I would have the bad one to fall back on. There is the possibility that the tumor could start growing and attack the good eye. I can see, I can drive and function just fine. God has been so good to me. I know He can open the eye in a blink and I will have perfect vision. I'll wait on Him. I will be still and know He is God. (Psalm 46:10). He is in control and will provide what I need.

ANOTHER ENCOUNTER WITH GOD

My sister was very ill and under hospice care. Her husband had been caring for her, but I went for a visit, to give him a rest. Every night, my sister and I would talk about our childhood, and what dying would be like. Our daddy died eighteen days before she was born. Would she finally see him? We talked a lot about what Jesus would be like. We both knew He loved us very much.

Every night, I would put her to bed and then I would sleep on a twin bed in the room with her. After I laid down, I would pray and listen for her even and steady breathing. I prayed that Jesus would take her gently. On July 3rd, 2010 at 4:15 PM, I gave her the medicines prescribed. I kissed her, and we said our good nights and *"I love you."* I laid down on my bed, but there was no long prayer time. No long listening to her breathe. I went to sleep immediately. About 45 minutes later, I woke up. I listened for her breathing and there was no sound. I knew then that God had made me sleep so I wouldn't be awake when she took her last breath. He took her gently, so I wouldn't awaken. I know she is in heaven and that I will see my baby sister again. God is so good. Now she has been united with my mom and dad and one day I will join them there.

*"All authority in heaven and on earth has been given to me. Therefore go and make disciples of all nations, baptizing them in the name of the Father and of the Son and of the Holy Spirit, and teaching them to obey everything I have commanded you. And surely, I am with you always, to the very end of the age." **Matthew 28: 18-20***

Dan's notation:

Thus, ends this the first chapter of *A Piece of Pie*. This first chapter shows us that God is real; that God *is*. He is there in times of uncertainty, in times of distress, in time of death and in times of joy. He is always there to give love, compassion, comfort, and forgiveness. He often sends His angels to encourage and inform us. If you, dear reader, are blessed with an angel visitation, please remember He who sent them.

Dan Cassidy and many others

Chapter Two

Redemption and Deliverance

*"Come to me, all you who labor and are burdened, and I will give you rest. Take my yoke upon you and learn from me, for I am gentle and humble of heart; and you will find rest for your souls. For my yoke is easy, and my burden light." **Matthew 11:28-30***

TESTIMONY OF A FOURTEEN-YEAR-OLD

I grew up not knowing my father. He wasn't the best influence in my life, so I wasn't able to see him. I have not seen him in many years. Now growing up without a father is the greatest thing that I have had to endure. I was able to see him for about a year, but it was all cut off like a light switch.

I have grown up in Clear Mountain Community Church, which has been a great blessing to me. I don't know where I would be without church. Ever since I have been going there, God has put great men in place of my father. I really look up to these men, because they have really shown me what it is like to be a man and how to always keep on the path of righteousness and not stray off. Straying off will lead to many problems.

I have struggled with a lot of addictions, but the one that really hits home for me to talk about is pornography. It has destroyed my life and has really distanced me from God and family. I would always think *doing it once can't hurt* or *I can just ask for forgiveness and it will all be taken away*. But I hear that does not work. That's the way I stopped doing it.

When my grandma died, I felt so broken, like I had nothing to do but be mad at God and question Him. Trust me; it isn't something you want to do. I would use pornography to fill the void of the loss. I thought it would make every bad and sad thought go away. It doesn't; it just makes it worse. I went on a mission trip and they had us break up in groups to get to know each other better. While I was in that group, I felt God just pulling on my heart to let it all out. I just started crying and told them about my addiction, and how I used it to fill the void of my grandma's death. It was a powerful talk.

A couple of months after that, I was talking to a guy and he had the same problem as me. I had no idea who he was. He just walked up to me and said, *"I feel like God has pointed me to you. I follow Him, and so I came to you. I feel like I need to pour out what God has told me to tell you about myself."* When we were done talking, we prayed, and I felt so different. I felt so alive and free, like a thousand pounds were lifted off my chest. That was the night God took away my addiction.

DRUG ADDICT FOUND

A grocery store clerk gave us this testimony about her niece. Her niece was addicted to drugs. One Sunday, her mother took her to church where she accepted the Lord as her savior. Suddenly, she fell to the floor. After she stood back up, she was taken off her feet again as she was being baptized by the Holy Spirit.

I heard this testimony some six weeks after the event. At that time, she was drug free.

The next time her aunt and I talked again was some months later, and she informed me that her niece was using again. May the good Lord bless and restore her once more.

A VETERANS TESTIMONY

As a US Army soldier, I have all the distinguished honor badges such as my Ranger Tab, Combat Infantry Badge, Expert Infantry Badge, and Air Assault Badge. I have been to numerous leadership schools, Sniper school, and other expert weaponry type courses. By the standards of the military, I am an excellent soldier, and have been awarded numerous military awards. I normally had more awards and badges than my superiors. I go the extra mile and at times, put myself in great danger in combat operations to protect our great soldiers and my superiors. In field training exercises, I would be the first one out of bed and the last one to go to sleep to ensure my soldiers were taken care of. In my worldly eyes, life was going well for me. That is, until I received a dreaded phone call from my brother, Mark. At that time, I had been in my 17th year of continuous Army service.

On July 30th, of the year 2000, my paternal father passed away at the early age of 52. He died quickly of a massive heart attack in the early morning hours at his home. Even though he was my father, he had never raised me at all. He was more like a fun, part-time dad, as I would go to his house during some school breaks and a portion of the summer. I never really could talk to him all that much, nor could I have a deep conversation with him at all. He was extremely quiet and very much an introvert. He was very proud of me for my Army service, as he was at my Basic Training graduation, and he was the one who pinned my Ranger Tab on my shoulder at my Ranger school graduation.

With a lot of issues never resolved with my dad, I was always reserved around him. The worst part of him dying was that I never heard him talk about God or Jesus. I was deeply bothered by the way he died because I was never sure if he cried out in his last breath to Jesus to be saved. Not to mention that I feel my dad and I never had the relationship I wish we could have had.

For six months after his death, I was at great loss. I felt sad for my dad for not knowing the Lord. I felt extremely cheated of the father-son relationship that I would have loved to have had. I had some deep questions to life's mysteries and was not satisfied with my life at all. I was also thinking that if I were to die, exactly where would I go? Would it be heaven or hell?

I decided one Sunday morning to get out of bed and drive around the city I lived in, to find a church. My son and I were sitting in a church parking lot and watching people enter the church. About 150 yards further down the road, there was another church where people were entering as well. I decided to start my pickup and drive to the other church. My son and I were greeted with such a warm welcome and everyone was extremely friendly. We started going to church at this little Pentecostal church immediately, as the teaching and the preaching were exactly what

I needed. I loved it! I had been going to this church for only a couple of weeks when I had a *Road to Damascus* experience.

I was at work in my military uniform and decided to drive to a Hardee's fast food restaurant for lunch. I received my tray of food which was a soda, cheeseburger, and French fries. As I walked to a table to sit down and enjoy my lunch, I noticed two older gentlemen sitting at another table with their bibles open, conversing with one another. I purposely sat at the table next to them because I wanted to hear the Word of God. Within 30 seconds I got up from my table and asked if I could sit with them. I was spiritually hungry for anything I could learn.

After conversing for 15 minutes or so, they asked me if I ever received the Holy Spirit by speaking in unknown tongues. My immediate answer was that I had not. Now mind you, I was in my Army uniform with all my badges on my chest, not to mention I was a high-ranking enlisted man. That did not matter to me, as I needed more, and I felt I was about to have a life-changing experience. With the two gentlemen talking with me, I raised my hands and immediately spoke in unknown tongues at the table. I felt like I was in a different world, and to this day I could not tell you if other people were around us or not. It really doesn't matter as this experience was for me. My soul felt liberated and I had a certain peace about me that hadn't ever existed before. I felt like a new man and these kinds of experiences are for real. I was over joyous!

Upon going to the Pentecostal church the next Sunday, I told everyone about the experience I had at Hardee's. I went in for a cheeseburger and came out of the restaurant with much more. Even though I was just a babe in Christ, I convinced the pastor that we needed a Sunday school for the young adults. I immediately became the youth pastor and was so happy to teach the young generation; to not only watch them grow in the lord, but the experience also helped me learn the bible at an accelerated rate. I loved learning and teaching the Word of God.

After my Hardees experience, I would occasionally go back to the restaurant to see if the older gentlemen were there. I wanted to sit and fellowship with them. Not once did I ever see them again at the restaurant. I feel they were angels in my life to help put me on the right track. I am so thankful for my angels. I am truly thankful for the experience they had brought me.

My life-changing experience has led me to a deeper understanding that our Father in heaven will never let us down, despite how even our closest relationships can fail us. I have learned that my biological father probably gave me as much as he knew how to give. I am at peace with that. The most important thing I have learned is that even though I am a Christian, I will continue to make mistakes. But by the Lord's grace and mercy I am forgiven for not only my past but my future as well. I will never give up hope. Every day is a blessed day and I am thankful that He entered my heart and gave me a heart transplant. A new one.

PASTOR MARK OTTEN

I was born in Cincinnati on June 30th, 1958, and moved to Milford, Ohio when I was two years old. I was part of a large Catholic family, and I attended Catholic schools for most of my childhood. I was one of 14 children that my parents raised and have always respected the values that I learned growing up in that environment. It instilled in me a respect for God, and His word. I was always taught to believe that the bible was the Word of God, and that truth would become a great benefit to me later in my life when I was confronted with the truth of the gospel. But when I began high school I rejected most of my parent's values, and I became immersed in the drug culture of the '70's. I got heavily involved in drugs and alcohol, and my all-consuming goal everyday was to find a way to get high. Most of my friends were also caught up in this same lifestyle, as we encouraged each other to go deeper and deeper into our sin and our destructive behaviors. By the time I was eighteen and out of high school, my substance abuse was skyrocketing, and my life was dedicated to getting high. There was something I was seeking for that the drugs and alcohol were not able to satisfy. I had an internal hunger and an inner desire for a life that had significance and purpose, but I was unable to find it. I was afraid and confused and my only escape was to get high.

God had a different plan for my life, and He wanted to free me from my bondage. My journey with God began shortly after my 18th birthday. My older brother, Bill, had just become saved and filled with the Holy

Spirit, and he experienced God in a way that I had never seen before. He too had been heavily involved with drugs and alcohol, but he had an experience with God that changed everything. Bill had been set free, and he wanted everyone to know about it. He was sharing the gospel with anyone who would listen, and that included me. I saw something in Bill that made me realize that he had found what I was looking for.

Then something else happened that shook my world. The girl I was dating had her own encounter with God. This beautiful girl, who would later become my wife, had surrendered her life to Christ, and was radically changed. She told me that she was saved, and had found something that was lasting and eternal, and would never let it go. The Jesus movement was sweeping through our town and young people everywhere were getting saved. This was a little bit too much for my Catholic mind to grasp, so I backed away from it and broke up with my girlfriend. But the damage had already been done. I had seen firsthand the reality of the new birth, and the Holy Spirit was dealing with my heart. Within a few weeks, I had surrendered my life to Christ and found the peace and rest that my weary soul had been longing for. I was instantly delivered from my addictions and my life was completely transformed. I discovered the purpose I was created for, a relationship with my maker. I fell in love with Jesus back in 1976 and I have never quit loving him.

I got back together with my girlfriend, Lisa, and the following year we were married. We moved from Milford, Ohio to Williamsburg, Ohio so that we could be more involved with the church that was being established there. Amazing things were happening in the church as the Holy Spirit was being poured out in our mist. Dozens of young people were getting saved and baptized in the Holy Spirit. We were seeing signs and wonders as people were getting healed and delivered. The gifts of the Holy Spirit were operating and there was a powerful presence of God in our worship services. We were *having church* as I had never known before.

As the years passed, and Lisa and I raised our three children, we continued to be involved in serving in ministry at our church. We were both teaching Sunday school classes, and I eventually got involved in youth ministry. As the church continued to grow, we labored and worked with our pastors through two building programs, and saw the church make a real impact in our community.

Lisa and I began working more closely with our pastors to disciple new believers, and we established a small group that met in our home. Later, I was asked to be on the board of the church and I served in that capacity for many years. When the founding pastor of the church retired, the new pastor restructured the church government, and asked me to be part of the leadership team as an elder, which I was happy to do.

Then in 2000, we merged with another full gospel church in town and we became Clear Mountain Community Church. I continued serving as an elder at Clear Mountain when our pastor suddenly *went home to be with the Lord* in December of 2003. It was a very difficult time for Clear Mountain Community Church, as we found ourselves without a pastor.

I began sharing from the pulpit with the other three elders, as we were seeking God for the direction of the church. As we were fasting and praying and searching for a new pastor to fill the vacancy, God confirmed his call on my life. He made it clear to me and the other elders that He had called me to the ministry. On January 9th, 2005, I left my business and was ordained as the pastor at Clear Mountain Community Church.

Since then, God has given us a vision at Clear Mountain to reach the next generation with the gospel of Jesus Christ. He's directed us to make sure we are effectively passing the gospel on to our children and grandchildren. He's led us to pour our time, energy, and resources into reaching the children and youth of our community.

God has helped us to raise up leaders that are making a real difference in the lives of our children and teens. We have established a highly effective children's ministry and youth ministry in our church. They are teaching our children and teens the uncompromising truth of our children's and youth ministries as more and more of them are being saved and baptized.

We are seeing Bible Clubs established in our schools, as more teens become hungry for God's word and want to take a stand for Christ. God has been faithful to honor what we've sown into the next generation, and we are seeing many new, young families becoming established in the church. He's also blessed us with beautiful mature, seasoned believers that have caught our vision, and are willing to invest their time, energy and resources into the next generation. We have seen some wonderful growth as we have moved from an average of about 200 people on Sunday morning to more than 400 attending.

In 2015, we could pay off the mortgage that once stood about 1.5 million dollars when I first took over as pastor in 2005. God has truly blessed us, and we are now debt free. We celebrated with a mortgage burning in January. To God goes the glory! We celebrated by donating $10800 towards the completion of an orphanage in Bulgaria. Yes, we are celebrating, but we also know we have much work to do in the harvest field. There are many in our community that are lost and have never received the love and forgiveness that Jesus offers.

We also know that we are called to make a greater impact in the mission field. Last year we sowed over $50,000 in to the mission field, and this year we will contribute more than $70,000. Jesus is coming soon, and it is time to bring in the harvest! We believe the best days of the church are still ahead, and we fully expect to see a great move of the Holy Spirit in these end times. We look forward to our Savior's soon coming, and we say *"Maranatha,"* come quickly Lord Jesus!

REBIRTH

I'm sure that writing this will be beneficial to me, as well as you, because we don't regret the past nor wish to shut the door on it. My testimony starts out at a young age when I went to church with my family. I learned about God and knew about Jesus, but the term *being saved* or *born again* never came up as far as I can remember. When we moved from New Jersey and started going to a different church, I didn't like the Sunday school and would rather sit in on the adult sermon. Some of it was interesting, but some of it was also boring, and I did a lot of day dreaming. What I heard never really related to Jesus or what He did for us on the cross.

When I was 12, my parents stopped making me go to church and let me stay home like I wanted. That was when my life took a turn for the worse, although it didn't seem like it at the time. I was already listening to Rock and Roll music and watching scary movies on TV. I was looking at Playboy magazines and cussing. I was smoking cigars and cigarettes by 14. I was drinking alcohol by 15, and smoking pot by 16. Things only became worse from there. When I joined the army, my dog tags stated no religious preference, which really means no preacher would come pray over you if you did get shot. I was using a cuss word in every sentence and smoking pot and drinking nearly every day. It *would* have been every day if I could.

My first wife left me in 1989. My new girlfriend, who I had known for about a month, came to me and said she was pregnant. She didn't know what to do. I told her to get an abortion. I am so glad that she didn't. I decided I should step up to the plate and marry her and take care of her and the baby for the rest of our lives. She was so hard to live with, and it's a wonder we stayed together as long as we did. We got married when my oldest daughter was four years old. She had another baby girl in 2002. When my youngest was three years old, my second wife decided she was going to take me for everything I have. She filed a protection order and had me thrown out of my house with no visitation rights to my daughters.

That's when I quit drinking and smoking and started going to Alcoholics Anonymous. Even after my lawyer proved that my second wife had lied to get the protection order, I was still out of there with no visitation rights. I was hitting bottom. I would be in Wal-Mart and see other families and their kids and I would have to go to the next aisle because I would start crying. Things seemed so hopeless. I found out from my neighbor that my wife had a boyfriend who was a short, skinny kid. He was in his early 20's. My lawyer suggested that I hire a private investigator. I found one on my own, because the lawyer was no help. The lawyer was the kind that drags his feet. The private investigator was good. He knew everything that was going on with my wife and daughters. The PI found out right away who the boyfriend was. He is a white supremacist with "white power" tattooed on the back of his bald head and "hate" tattooed on his chest. He had also been in prison and was wanted in a nearby town. Even though my private investigator had all this information and was uncovering new information week by week, the court was still not interested. We would go to court and nothing would happen. We would set up a meeting. At the meeting, we would set a court date, and on and on it went.

In the meanwhile, I had gained visitation rights and had supervised visitation with my parents where I had been living. Every week was a celebration! I decided that I should take my daughters to church. My neighbor suggested one and we went. It was a real eye opener for me. My daughters liked it too. When I asked my youngest if she liked it, she said *"Yeah, can we go tomorrow?"* We went every Sunday, and we still do. I was learning a lot, and where the bible once didn't make sense to me, now it was making perfect sense. I decided to lay down my old sinful life and give my new life to Jesus. Things were starting to look up. I had a much better outlook. My lawyer suggested that my wife and I have psychiatric evaluations. We did, and the report ruled in my favor. Her lawyer suggested we get a *Guardian Ad Litem*, which is a lawyer for the welfare of the kids and is used by both parties involved. I spilled my guts to this *Guardian Ad Litem* and she ended up ruling in my favor. We went to court for the last time, and came to an agreement before court, so we didn't have a hearing. I got full custody of my kids with child support and I got my home back. It's because I hung in there and kept on praying. I give full credit to God. He saved my life. He allowed me to go through hard times to bring me to Him for His perfect purpose and glory. Amen! Amen! My life has never been better.

A BLIND MAN HELPS ME SEE

My name is Leroy and I grew up in Augusta, Maine. My mom and dad were fine Christians and they did the best they could to provide for six children. We did not have much, but we were loved, and we always knew that. I was the prodigal son and always hated school. I did very well in school *when I went*, but I skipped a lot.

I resented that we never had much money and dad always tithed to God and it didn't seem to me that Mom and Dad were rewarded for their faithfulness. So, I couldn't wait to get away from home, so I wouldn't have to go to church each time the doors opened.

I got married when I was 17 years old to my wife of 60 years now. The first 15 years were so hard on my wife. We had six children by the time I was 29, and I had become a miserable person to live with. Why my wife stayed with me, I will never know, but she took her wedding vows seriously and put up with my drunkenness and mental abuse. I left our home several times, and she always took me back. We had moved to Florida and had lived there for eight years. It was a terrible eight years for her, but she stuck it out until the last time I left our home. I was gone for about a month. My wife took the children and moved back to Maine. After a month or so, she had settled back in Maine. My Mom got in contact with me in Florida and told me my wife and family still loved me, to come home, and that God still loved me and would forgive me. Well, I came back to Maine wondering why anyone would want anything to do with a worthless drunk like me, but they welcomed me with open arms. My wife was going to church every week with the kids and I had cut back on my drinking, so things were a little better.

One day, my wife said they were having a gospel quartet singing at the church, and I love music, so I went to church with her *just for the music*, I thought. The leader of the group was in a wheelchair, and at the end of the service he gave his testimony of how he grew up in a fine Christian home. He had contracted polio and could not move. He was in an iron lung for a long time. He ended up unable to move from the waist down. He blamed God and was bitter for a long time. Like me, he had gone to church to hear the gospel quartet because he loved music. After the music, the preacher preached, and he was blind. He told of how he had been in a sledding accident when he was 16 years old, and had been blind ever since. Then he told of how God blesses his life just the same and had used him just the way he was. The man in the wheelchair said he realized that the blind man saw more with his blind eyes than he saw with his good eyes, so he gave his life to Jesus.

Well, I knew right then that these two men had what I had been running from my whole life. I came to the altar and gave my life to Jesus, and I experienced a miracle in my life, one that I never imagined. I have never since craved a smoke or a drink, and my language has changed. I love my family in a way I never had before. I cannot imagine where I would be if I had not turned my life over to Jesus. Or where my family would be. I've had a wonderful life, I loved Jesus with all my heart. I owe all that I have become to Him.

Dan's notation:

The theme of this chapter is the life changing power of Christ. All the people in this chapter experienced a life changing encounter with the Lord. God used their brokenness, interests, and other people to lead them to the place and time where they were ready to receive Jesus. God is in control, and He alone has the power to change us all for the better. He sometimes uses people to help in His efforts. You may be the one who He chooses to help another in their walk. Give a word of encouragement, be an example, a helping hand. Each of these men freed from the chains that bonded them were given new lives through Christ Jesus.

Ask and it will be given to you; seek and you will find; knock and the door will be opened to you. For everyone who asks receives; he who seeks finds; and to him who knocks, the door will be opened. ***Matthew 7:7-8***

Dan's notation:

The next testimony is from a vocal testimony given in a church setting.

A STORY OF FAITH, HOPE, AND LOVE
Jeff and Suzanne Coulter's Story

Jeff's Story

We attend Clear Mountain Community Church in Williamsburg, Ohio, the town where I grew up, and we take part in local ministries where God needs us. My wife is originally from West Virginia, but grew up in Ohio, just west of Williamsburg.

We married in September of 1987. To put that into perspective, we still had phone booths back then, no internet, and cell phones the size of bricks. We met just four months prior in May of the same year. When God moves, He moves fast! We fell madly in love with each other and never wanted to be apart again.

Our main ministry is our books that we share over global media, and we have recently started appearing at speaking engagements. Back in the day, when Clear Mountain Community Church was The Williamsburg Pentecostal Church, it was always a blessing to have "Teen Challenge" (a faith-based organization dedicated to helping troubled young people) at the services praising God in the front three pews.

What I want to talk to you about now is redemption. What it means to me, and that it is available to all of us who have an open and sincere heart. God has made His redemption available to all of us, no matter what the sin is in our lives, and no matter what our mindset may be. Whether you think that you are lost and past the point of no return, I'm here to tell you today that God's redemption is available to you every minute of every day.

I became saved when I was seven years old and was brought up in church ever since that day. In 1988, my world changed when I lost my mother to cancer. She and I were very close, and we prayed together often. Soon after her death, I began to lose my faith and walked away from God. I suppose deep down inside I blamed God, even though I never did so openly. I entered into a profound chronic depression.

I had fallen away from God, and soon began to look for something to fill the giant void that I created once I removed God from my everyday life. One day, God spoke to me and said to me, *"You cannot serve two masters. You will either hate the one and love the other. If you are lukewarm, I will spew you out of my mouth."* But instead of listening, I decided to run farther away.

I started to drink, and my drinking became worse and more pronounced. I would brag about the pyramids of beer cans that I would create over the weekend. I fell into sin and the Devil's grasp. I was in and out of church but never seriously committed myself to God. I just went through the motions while I was backsliding.

It was my choice. I could have changed it at any time, but I no longer wanted anything to do with anything. I just wanted to forget.

I started living for the moment and only focused on hedonism and carnal gratification. I just wanted to get drunk and stay numb. I began to leave my wife at home and go to the lake, so I could fish and drink and have a good time. I neglected the most important people in my life. My marriage was on the verge of collapse. My wife and I separated, and I moved in to my own apartment. This was not just a midlife crisis, this was attempted escapism. I was trying to run away from God, my family, and myself.

By God's grace, my wife and I managed to reconcile to the point where I moved back in to the house. But even after everything that I was going through, I still didn't get it. I still couldn't see the forest for the trees. However, God is a faithful and just. He does not forget His elect. He calls us His own and we are His children.

On April 22nd, 2014, I decided to go fishing about a ten-minute drive up the road, at a nice fishing hole called Tunnel Mill. A car coming from the opposite direction went left of center on a blind hill and hit me head on. I had time enough to blink, but not much else.

My car went into a spin, and when it stopped, I couldn't breathe. I had the wind knocked out of me from the impact. All I could say was *okay, okay, okay*, until I got my breath. *Jesus! Jesus! Jesus!* I cried. I kept looking over at the passenger seat, and even though I couldn't physically see anyone, I felt the presence of someone sitting next to me. You know that feeling when someone comes up behind you or invades your space? That's what I felt that day. There was someone sitting next to me that day, and His name was Jesus.

A calm came over me, and once I regained my senses, I tried to move. I was pinned under the dash, and when I tried to move the steering wheel, I realized that my arm was badly broken. I don't think that the strongest person could have done a better job swinging a baseball bat. My left forearm had snapped clean in two.

I looked for my phone, so that I could call my wife, but it had broken away from my belt clip and I couldn't find it anywhere. I just wanted to tell her that I loved her one last time. I tried to move the steering wheel with my good arm, but there was just no way. I was in public service for about 18 years and had a lot of training for shock, so I just leaned back and placed my arm on my chest and said to myself, *"Just stay calm, you'll hear the sirens soon. You are close to town."* There, I just bowed my head and prayed.

Only a few minutes after I started praying, people started gathering around the car. The first one was a person calling emergency services. Then the second person was a Baptist preacher. I can't think of a more welcome sight than those two people after you've been involved in a head-on collision.

The Baptist preacher checked on me and saw that I was praying. He asked me, *"Are you a believer?"* I nodded my head and he prayed with me. Then the fire department arrived and asked him to move away. After about an hour of cutting me loose from the car, I was in a helicopter en route to the UC trauma center.

Fast forward to after multiple surgeries, and I was on the fast track to recovery. Even though I was patched back together from a shattered hip, a broken arm, broken foot, ribs and a knee cap, I was still not seeing the big picture. These were my last moments on Earth and I couldn't see the writing on the wall.

After moving to an inpatient hospital room, they were already talking about discharging me. While sitting and talking with my wife, I suddenly passed out in her arms. The next thing I knew, I awoke to a room full of medical staff. I had multiple blood clots travel to my heart and lungs. My body had stopped on a dime. My brain said *so long* to my organs, and I was dying.

I am told that my heart rate had more than doubled, at 180 bpm, and that my blood pressure was nearly cut in half at 88/30. For any pumping system, that is a sure sign of an issue. I slipped into unconsciousness and began to see the other side as I felt my spirit start to slip away. Right before I was taken back to intensive care, I remember trying to calm down, but I just couldn't make my heart slow down. I was under extreme duress and couldn't do anything to stop it. I looked at my wife and also my daughter and began to speak in tongues, and I said *goodbye* to both of them. Suzy looked at me and yelled; *"Don't you dare leave me!"*

I went to a place where there was no presence of God. A complete and utter absence of the presence of the very God who binds the world together. I've never felt fear so pure in my life and trust me, I've been on the wrong side of a lot of scary things. I cried out to Jesus but there was no answer. I looked for God in the darkness, but He was nowhere to be found.

I could hear the growls and laughter of the demons of Hell. I was going down the dark tunnel literally scared to death! Then much like the Baptist preacher appeared at the crash scene, my mother appeared in front of me. She looked me in the eye, and I woke up in the hospital room again. It was surreal. I was looking around to make sure that it was over.

I'm never going to forget the pure terror and loneliness that I felt. You know that feeling you get when you wake up from a nightmare? This was a real nightmare. By that I don't mean "really" I mean "real" as real as any other experience I have had in my life.

I repented of my sin over and over to God and begged Him for his forgiveness and salvation! After the trauma center stabilized my condition, and after being in intensive care for a month, I was finally able to go home. I have rededicated my life to Christ: my Father and my King.

You see when you are God's elect, it doesn't matter how long you've been away from His saving grace. Time and distance have no meaning to God. He is everywhere and all-knowing. He knew that this crash was going to happen, and he knew that I would call out to Him. One old Hymn has a lot of meaning to me these days.

He was there all the time.

He was there all the time.
Waiting patiently in line.
He was there all the time.

The Chief Surgeon came in at the end of my recovery and told me point blank to my face; *"My staff and I don't know how you are here."* Without hesitation I told him, *"God gave me another day."* Even though I looked the other way, God was there for me with His loving and tender mercy.

I am here to tell you today that this is the purpose that God has for me and my wife: to be witnesses to His glory and His redemption. His forgiveness and His salvation. I'm here today to tell you that it doesn't matter how deep you are in the hole, there is always light at the end of the tunnel. God will pull you out of the darkness and show you the light.

If you feel trapped by the grips of addiction or condemnation over your past, and don't think that there is any way out, I'm here to tell you that you are wrong. **2 Corintjhians 5:17** says, *"Therefore if anyone is in Christ, he is a new creation: the old has gone, the new has come!"*

I'm also thankfully here to tell you that you don't have to have a head-on crash to find the answer. It doesn't have to come to a life or death event to bring you back to the Father. After nearly 25 years of living in sin, God forgave me. He offered to me His infinite redemption even after all of those years of rejecting Him. God's word says that all of us have sinned and fall short of the Glory of God. So, you are not alone, and you are not singled out. Most of all, He is always there for you as long as you have a humble heart.

Don't forget the story of the *Prodigal Son*. He had to hit absolute rock bottom and eat with the swine before he came back to his father. His father didn't spurn him or tell him that he was unwelcomed; he welcomed him back with open arms and killed the fatted calf, celebrating his return. Today, Jesus has taken me back into His loving arms. He has killed the fatted calf and is celebrating my return as one of His children.

Think of all these things that I've told you today. The story doesn't end here. My wife Suzanne would like to talk to you about her faith. While I was still recuperating, and she was still taking care of me, we received a call from Suzy's mother in the middle of the night. A phone call from any family member in the middle of the night is never a good thing, but this call would push Suzy's faith to the very edge.

SUZY'S STORY

I grew up with one sibling. My brother Danny was born 13 months after me and even though we were close together in age, we were not close in other ways while growing up. He was born with a cleft palate and a cleft lip, so he was up against it from the get-go. With the help of major surgeries from the time he was an infant until he was an adult, his physical disability was minimized to a certain degree, but the effects on his emotional health were long-lasting.

As a young child he was bullied because of his physical differences and this led him to choose some less than desirable friends. He started smoking cigarettes around the age of 10 and this eventually led him to smoking marijuana, later doing harder drugs as a teenager.

He made some very bad choices, one of which was stealing our parents' 1970 Mustang and running away to West Virginia. He didn't even have a driver's license yet, but apparently had been rolling the car out of the garage and joy riding with friends in the middle of the night for a very long time before this. After he was located at a relative's house in West Virginia, my parents made the tough decision to have him arrested and brought back to Cincinnati, Ohio, to stay in a halfway house until some very important behavioral issues could be resolved.

We all participated in family counseling while he was living away from home, and we made a lot of progress to help deal with the issues in the family. Danny eventually came back home to live, but still struggled with his grades in school, and with drug and alcohol abuse. He was able to graduate from high school, after which he entered the United States Air Force, where he served for many years.

He married while he was stationed in the Philippines and he had four children: one girl who died right after birth, and three boys. He continued to struggle with addiction in the form of cigarette smoking, which he quit for a while before going back to it, but had given up any drug abuse when he entered the Air Force. After he got out of the Air Force, he had a successful technical career, and eventually started his own business to supplement his income from employment.

Several physical things pained Danny in addition to the ones he was born with: he hurt his back while he was still in the Air Force, and he had a very severe motorcycle accident several years after his honorable discharge. These physical ailments led to horrible pain and many surgeries, and of course, prescription pain medication.

Because of Danny's history of drug addiction, it was inevitable for him to become hooked on the prescription pain medicines, which is exactly what happened. Eventually no amount of medication could ease his pain and he feared being in a wheelchair, not able to financially support himself and his wife, and becoming a burden for her to care for.

His three boys were grown by this time, two of them were married, and one was expecting his first child in August of 2015. Danny was over the top excited at the announcement of his first grandchild in November of 2014, but he soon began to dwell on his physical limitations in terms of playing with and holding his grandchild.

His pain, fueled by the fact that the pain medications were not easing his pain anymore, and the doctors who were not prescribing anything to help him, led him to take his own life by gunshot to the head in January of 2015.

Danny struggled with physical ailments his entire life, and these physical ailments led to chemical abuse in several different forms throughout his life. He was trying to cover his physical and emotional scars with substance abuse, and eventually it just wasn't enough to ease the pain.

Unfortunately for all of us left behind, we now have a pain that nothing will ever take away. My belief and faith and trust in God is the only thing that eases that pain in any way.

I encourage all of you to keep looking up. God is looking down. He is always there for you and never will condemn you. Never forget this simple prayer when you are up against a struggle, "God help me please." Just continue to show God your sincere heart and always remember that He loves you so much that He gave the life of His son. He loves us so much.

Let's bow our heads.

"Father in Jesus wonderful name thank you for the opportunity to speak to your children today. Please bless them and keep them safe. Thank you for your redemption and thank you for the sacrifice of your Son Jesus. We ask your blessings and divine protection over all of your children. Walk with them daily and keep them encouraged, my Master and my Father. Let them feel your presence each and every day, and may they always feel your presence and never feel like they're without hope. In Jesus wonderful name, I pray. Amen."

DYSFUNCTIONAL FAMILY TO GOD'S FAMILY

I am twenty-seven years old. I have thought for months about what I was going to write about my short life. The question I have asked myself has been where to start? Do I talk about the day I remember letting god into my life as an adult, or giving up on him as a child? You see; when I was young, I was raised Catholic, so I knew God, and I loved him from a very young age. I remember going to Sunday school with my Nana and reading books about Jesus and the song *this little light of mine*. I remember it all. Unfortunately, I remember the hurt, the pain and the anger that I had for everyone around me. I knew about all the injustices my mother and father and others have inflicted on me. People who should have protected my brother and I.

I remember being about six years old and playing with my two younger brothers. We were constantly in trouble. The earliest memory I have of my mother and father together is when we were living in an apartment in Oakland Beach. My mother had locked me in a hot room on the second floor on a hot summer day.

My father came home from work and beat her down for it. He was not the only abuser though. You see, mother dearest liked to play the victim, but she usually started it. Another time they were drunk or high and got into it. My little brother and I were playing with the wet paint on the wall. My father took us by our throats and threw us down the stairs into a wall. That night was not even the worst case of domestic violence that we endured. That night after he threw us down the stairs, Mother made us walk for hours and told everyone about what happened. She loved the attention instead of calling for help and maybe getting us a safe bed to sleep in, she paraded our hurt for what would be classified as todays' "likes" on social media.

I believe he went to jail for a while for that. Then the state got wind of it and that's when even more of our life started sucking. My brothers and I were taken away for a while. Separated, of course, by the state, my first night in a foster home, I cried for my mommy. I remember the foster parents saying, *Stop crying you little brat! Your mom is not coming! No one is coming!* I hated that foster family. You know the ones that do it only for the money, that don't care.

Once you become a state kid, you have it rough. When you get moved, the stuff you own is garbage, it's in a garbage bag that is what they give you. You technically have nothing to call your own. There are no after school activities or sleep-overs at friends or at church. No church: that wasn't allowed.

Our mother got us back after that one, but that did not stop her games of course. The games and the fact that she always needed a man. She could never be single this lady; like seriously get your life together! It was like an escalator of men, one after the other. The state told me that I had been molested as a younger child. I probably was, but if I was, I don't remember it at all, thank Jesus for that.

The state has a file on me and my family, and my son; patient's history they call it but it's my family history. I would love to get my hands on it, so I can tell them all the parts that are fabricated and false. My parents were addicts, and to this day do not personally think that addiction is an illness. My background is in health care, and as a nursing student, I know that it is, but I can't make myself believe it. Addicts are liars and love to play the victim and use the people that are around them for their own sick purposes. They never apologize because it's a "disease."

When I have patients who are addicts, I just have no sympathy. Because of my past. I will have to come to terms with the past on my own. Addiction is the devil in his most natural form. All compassion just shuts off in my brain, and to me that's natural and I'm okay with it. I am protecting me, it's what I must do.

Today I don't have to defend myself and who I am, people know already. But my past has me constantly protecting something that does not need protecting. I am loved, cherished, believed in, and have an army behind me. I know what it's like to be alone, but I am constantly sabotaging relationships. It like hey *this is me crazy can you handle it or just leave* I can do it alone. My husband is amazing, and he deals and loves the crazy. Only God could have created the perfect man for me, but more about him later.

Now with all that I have been through with my incompetent parents, being a teen mother, and in an abusive relationship, I should be an extremely mean person, hateful even, and at times I can be, but I'm not. I guard myself well because the people that should have taken care of me, loved me, nurtured me failed miserably at their job. In their job to raise a woman, they failed.

Everyone thought I was going to end up the drug addicted prostitute, but I didn't. I was angry, nasty, mean. I had very few friends until I became as low as I thought that I could be. I finally cut off a six year, highly abusive relationship, and that left my son and I alone. My damaged son. My damaged self, that I allowed my son to see me abused, that heard me verbally abuse others because of how I felt, and how I hurt on the inside. My son suffered, and when I look back, I believe I did the best I could because chaos, hate, hurt, and abuse was all I had ever learned and known, so it was what was normal to me.

Until my son started acting out behaviorally to the point that I couldn't get anyone to babysit him. In order to work, I had to use his biological father's family, who were, to me, not interested in protecting my son's innocence regarding life at all. They allowed him to watch R-rated movies, and to hear things that a kid shouldn't hear. But what could I do when I had to work; to provide, to pay rent, buy food? I did what I had to do, but we suffered. Everyone told me that I was a good mom, but I didn't think so.

Who stays in a relationship where the man hits you in front of your child? Who stays in a relationship consisting of yelling, fighting, and cussing? Who stays? The person who thinks they are not deserving of love. The person who thinks extremely little of themselves. there were good times with that man, but it was 80% bad. He cheated repeatedly, and I would still take him back. We were toxic to each other, and we became toxic to my son.

Then, at work, a woman told me about her church and that I was invited to go if I ever wanted to. Why would this woman care about me when I was so mean and angry to everyone all the time? Why me? I was the girl that never cried, never showed any emotion other than anger. Then, I broke up with him again. The police became involved again, but this time something changed in me. I went to church on Wednesday, September 12th, 2012, to a young adult's service. The pastor was preaching on my now favorite verse, **Proverbs 4:23**. *Above all else guard your heart for everything you do flows from it.* The atmosphere of the room, the love I felt while I was there, and I have never left. I remember the smell of that day, the feeling I had of relief, of safety, of stability, the feeling of being truly loved. I had it in that day, in that moment. Following that day, I started going to church, every Wednesday at first.

I went to my first retreat. I hated the guest speaker, so I was mad all weekend, wanted to go home as the Pastor knew. But the last day, the last service, something happened in me and that was the day that I believe I accepted Christ as my lord and savior. I remember the feeling, I remember the smell, and I mostly remember the love that I felt. This was when the devil started his games with me and he still plays the games today.

My step father was in jail and my biological mother moved back in to the apartment with me and my son. We had attempted to move in with my biological dad, to get through nursing school, which would help me with babysitting and would help him financially. I didn't know that he was a racist, and my son is half black. He called my son a *jigga boo* which means *nigger*. A black neighbor heard him and punched out his bottom teeth. My dad then turned around and threw me across the bathroom by my throat, in front of my son.

This abuse lasted two whole days and then I moved in with my stepdad. My mother then moved back in with my stepfather and made me lie to my stepfather about her having a new guy move in, about what she was doing, so she was able to get everything in the divorce that she filed for.

She then left two months later without paying any bills and took everything from us. All that was left in the apartment were my things and his clothes. I tried to continue with these toxic relationships with my parents, but it was obvious I was the parent in the relationship. The child was the parent. My pastors advised me for months to let them go, but it's hard. I had been raised in state care. I really had no one. I would spend Christmas and thanksgiving with friends I met in college, or co-workers, before I met my church family.

One day though, my mother finally threatened me, and I went ballistic on her. The things I said to her she honestly deserved and more, but I regret how I said them.

It was that day that I grew in my walk and my life. I cut all ties with my parents. It was the hardest thing that I had ever done but then I was able to focus on something more important, my son, and myself. At this point my stepdad had gotten out of jail and came home. He was considering going back to my mother even after everything she had done. Once again, the devil is a liar.

I moved out and got my own apartment alone again. My son's behavior was now out of control, so I had to seek professional help, and he ended up in intensive inpatient treatment for ten months. Now this was the hardest thing that I had ever done. When I would come home from work it would be to an empty house. My baby was only ten, and he was gone. It shouldn't be like that.

The first month he was gone, I worked and drank a lot. I was suicidal, and the devil knew where he could hurt me the most. I look back and the alcohol was the reason the devil didn't get his ultimate reward of me taking my own life. I didn't go to church that month, but church came to me. My church family prayed over me and for me and they helped Jesus win.

After I got over that empty nest feeling, I started working on myself with my son's family therapist and I went to parent support groups. My stepdad got back together with my mother, so I had to also cut him out of my life. All my parents were toxic to have relationships with. They still are to this day. When I finally cut out all of these people who were dragging me down, keeping me angry, I was then able to focus on myself and what I needed to be a better person and mother. Jesus is who did that. In the time my son was a patient, I had a major transformation myself. I literally woke up one day and decided that these people that hurt me, those that had a hold on me, would never have control or a say in my life again. I deleted all worldly people from my phone and social media. I took the time I now had alone and worked on me.

I figured out why I was so angry. I was mistreated by social workers, foster parents and family, but it was all over. I was angry because I had not forgiven yet. When a person finds Christ and joins a church, you cannot expect them to have their life in order right away. It took me a while to figure it out, but I did, and it was my choice. Now, forgiveness is not given because the person being forgiven deserves it, it's given for yourself. God forgives you for all you have done so you need to forgive others; if not for them, then for you, because you are worth it. God gave his life for you, the least you can do to return the favor is forgive others of their transgressions, and one day maybe someone also can forgive you. Now forgiving others wasn't the hardest part: it was forgiving myself.

I still struggle at times with forgiving myself, but it's because I am my own biggest critic. But I do forgive me. Doing that allowed me to focus on fixing what needed to be fixed with my family and myself.

I met an amazing man seven months into my son's treatment, and we moved to Maine, engaged three months later, and started this next chapter of life. I have been married for two years, in nursing school, and my son is thriving because God chased me down. I fell in love with Jesus. I found the filling to the empty space in my life that I was feeling. It was all Jesus. I know now, however, that he put me through so much, and this testimony does not even go deep but Jesus put me through all my trials, so I would be able to share with others and help them.

Hopefully, in less than a year I will have graduated nursing school and my husband, and our son and I will be doing amazing. We are normal now. We are stable and comfortable and it's all because of Jesus. We don't have a million dollars, but we found love, stability, and now I do have a family. God had helped me through so much so that when I got to the good stuff, I could appreciate it more.

Without God I probably would have become a drug addict prostitute, but I didn't. Instead, I'm a wife, mother, nursing student, daughter-in-law, sister, and I am worth it because God chose me.

Dan's notation:

God has not only saved this young woman from her troubled past, He has broken the chain of family abuse and drug addiction. He has, in my opinion, transformed her into one of the kindest, biggest hearted people I have ever met.

Chapter Three

Healing

*The blind receive sight, the lame walk, those who have leprosy are cured, the deaf hear, the dead are raised, and the good news is preached to the poor. **Matthew 11:5***

HEALING TESTIMONY

In the mid 1990's, I was diagnosed with crippling arthritis in my hands, wrists and elbows. My joints were large and inflamed, my fingers began twisting, and it was very painful. I worked in maintenance and could barely work or hold anything without dropping it. We were praying and believing for my healing.

I went to a hand specialist. At that time, we had some of the finest hand specialists in the country here in Cincinnati. They ran me through every test they had. They told me there was nothing that could be done medically. They said I would have to start taking prescription pain medications. They also said I would need stronger and stronger prescriptions over time. The symptoms became increasingly worse. While sitting in a meeting and listening to a teaching on spiritual warfare, I felt the Holy Spirit go into both arms at the same time, down through my elbows, wrists, and through my hands. The next morning the strength had returned to my hands.

I was completely healed by the power of God and prayer, and do not have any more pain or problems.

THE LORD HAS HEALED ME

While traveling with three other men to see the natural bridge in Kentucky, I told Marvin that I have a minor back problem. It was just a sticking feeling, as if the discs were not moving freely. For the record, I had and still have more serious back problems, but the only one I mentioned to Marvin was the sticking problem. I learned a valuable lesson that day, ask not and you will receive not, if ever I am asked if someone can pray over me for healing, I will be sure to mention everything, including the cavities in my teeth. God always listens, and it could be that this would be the time He will give you all you ask. Marvin, I found out later, is a minister and had a healing ministry in my home town.

He asked if he could pray for my healing. I said, *"For sure,"* and he did. The next day, I noticed the feeling was gone. I told Marvin and he said, *"In thirty years and countless healings, no one had ever said 'The Lord God has healed me.' Thanks be to God. Alleluia!"*

I told him I would I would, assuming it would be in a church setting. One week later, I did repeat the words Marvin had given me. It was on that weekend that I was baptized, by immersion, in my home church. As I stood on the alter, I asked the pastor if I could say a few words. He said I could. I said *"The Lord God has healed me. Thanks be to God. Alleluia."*

These words became my testimony. The testimony of a Holy Spirit encounter, at a men's retreat, during which I received the message that *time is short*, and the healing of the sticking feeling in my back, delivered at what I call my adult baptism.

HEAD INJURY

At the urging of several people from our church knowing that I have chronic diseases, my husband, Dan, and I attended a service led by a healer. My husband and I had discussed me requesting healing of a chronic disease. While there, I volunteered to approach the healer. I had requested healing from epilepsy. However, God had another plan. The healer touched me on the head and shoulders and asked if I had an injury to my head recently. I had a severe headache at that time. I had fallen the previous weekend. No one knew of my injury, my husband and I had told no one. The fall had caused a concussion. The healer prayed for my healing, and my headache and the other signs of the concussion were gone. He also asked if there was anything else. At that time, I had a pain in my foot from repeated injuries. I told him it was nothing, really thinking that other people had a greater need than I, with my sore foot. He replied that there is nothing too small for God.

Prayer was offered, and my foot was also healed.

YES YOU

While attending a revival many years ago, there was a young Jewish man conducting the service. He was laying on hands and praying with people, and the Lord was healing them. He suddenly stopped and asked for the man with the eye problem to stand up. I just sat, believing he was speaking to someone else. Then he looked right at me and said *yes, you.* Somewhat surprised that he singled me out, I did as he asked. He prayed over me and then I sat back down, not feeling any different. At the end of the night, my friend who had driven me there was taking me home, for over the years, this senior's vision had declined to the point that I could no longer drive myself at night. About half way home, I complained that I could not see. Everything was distorted until I removed my glasses, after which I could see clearly. The Lord had restored my eye sight.

YEAH GOD!

What God did for me!

I stay amazed at the Power of God! I had a "frozen shoulder" and could not lift my arm over my head. I had been for an x-ray and an MRI. The doctor said I could either have surgery or wait it out. It could take many months for it to work itself out.

My worship and praise are all (both) hands in the air. My new church is Holy Spirit–filled, which is new to me, even though I have been in the church all of my life.

We had a healing service, which was my first. I was worshipping but also sad because I could not lift both hands in the air. I asked the lord; *"Will I never be able to praise you with both hands again?"*

My pastor called those who needed healing up on the stage. My faith led me up there. He laid hands on me and I fell into the spirit. I felt as if I had a heart attack of love. I totally forgot what had happened. I lay weeping, my heart racing…but there was no fear, just love. When I recovered, I got up and walked off the stage, kind of bewildered but at peace. The worship team began to play and my hands went straight up to the heavens, both of them. It took me a minute to realize that I had been healed! When I jumped for joy and shared that I had been healed, there was minimal reaction. This is a church where the spirit moves often, and healings are not out of the norm. I was amazed, and *stay* amazed! Yeah God! If I had pompoms that said *YEAH GOD!* I would shake them all the time. So, if you ever hear a girl running around saying "Yeah God," it might be me.

Jesus reached out his hand and touched the man, "I am willing," he said, "Be clean!" Immediately he was cured of his leprosy.
Matthew 8:3

OUT OF THE ICU

It was in 2011 when our special needs son got sick and went to the hospital. He had cerebral palsy seizure disorder, was blind, and was on a feeding tube. He was also nonverbal, so he couldn't tell you what was going on. When he was born, we were told that he only had a five-year life expectancy. Even with these multiple handicaps, he was a very happy little guy.

In the hospital, we were told that he was septic, which is an infection in the blood often caused by a pathogenic organism of some kind. His numbers on the blood tests continued to get worse day by day. The tests found a mass or tumor, and the doctors removed it, as well as a testicle. Still his numbers decreased continuing to get worse. Four out of five doctors pretty much said there was nothing that they could do. They asked for a DNR – a legal written order not to resuscitate, and to withhold life support in the event of cardiac arrest – but we did not grant it. Only his primary care physician did not give up on our son.

His condition deteriorated to the point that they moved him to the ICU. Just as they got him settled and hooked up to all the machines, our pastor, Pastor Joseph, came by to pray over him. We had become accustomed to watching the numbers all the time. Just as our pastor prayed, I noticed the numbers started to change for the better. So much so that within two hours, they took him out of the ICU. Within two or three days, he was home and back to his old self.

When we returned to his primary care physician, we began to thank him for all he had done. He admitted that it wasn't he that changed the outcome, but that it was truly a miracle. *Someone* higher than he was responsible. We all know that *Someone* was the Lord Jesus Christ. Our son is now 28 years old and healthy as ever.

Dan's notation:

Before He was crucified, Jesus healed many. It should be no surprise to anyone that miraculous healings take place today. God never changes.

Jesus went throughout Galilee, teaching in their synagogues, preaching the good news of the kingdom, and healing every disease and sickness among the people. **Matthew 4:23**

Dan Cassidy and many others

Chapter Four

Physical Lives Saved

Then Moses stretched out his hand over the sea, and all that night the Lord drove the sea back with a strong east wind and turned it into dry land. The waters were divided. **Exodus 14:21**

Dan's notation:

This chapter seeks to show some of God's unlimited power over the natural world. The manner in which He has saved the lives of many people, my own included, demonstrates His power over all the natural laws. Gravity is cancelled, solid objects pass thru each other, cars move thru time and space. Human bodies can be hit by cars with only minor injuries. God created all the natural laws that seem to control the physical world, and He can change them, revoke them, or add to them in any way He chooses.

ON THE OTHER SIDE

This is the testimony of Dan E. regarding a supernatural experience I had in the late summer of 1987 or 1988.

I used to volunteer at a youth group called Colerain Breakfast Club. The youth were all students at my old high school. I helped run the group, led worship and discipled kids. I was 25 at the time.

I was driving to a discipling session one evening, down Hanley Road in White Oak, in the north-west suburbs of Cincinnati. I was running late to the meeting and was driving too fast. Hanley Road is almost perfectly straight, but, is very topographic, and the road hugs the side of a series of hills, often with a steep drop off on one side and a steep hill on the other.

I was approaching a dangerous section that had a steep drop off on one side and a hill on the other. Some houses had hidden driveways on the drop off side of the road, and you could crest a hill and suddenly there would be a car pulling out of one of those driveways.

That is what happened to me: I came over the most blind hill at around 50 miles per hour (Hanley is a 35 miles per hour zone), when a station wagon pulled out of one of those driveways and was blocking the entire width of the road from side to side.

I could not go around it because of the hillside – which was more of a cliff-side – blocked my left. There was no room there at all. To my right was a steep drop off, although there was a driveway there, from the angle that I was approaching, I would have rolled my car at least one hundred feet or more.

I had a split second to think, and that was it. I closed my eyes, muttered, *"Jesus,"* under my breath, and braced to hit the other car. I don't think I even hit the brakes, it happened that quickly.

I felt the steering wheel jerk, not to one side or the other, but as if I had hit railway tracks at a high speed. I could feel my hands vibrate for about a second or two. The next thing I knew, I was on the other side of the station wagon. It had not budged an inch. I was still perfectly in my lane. I *should have* hit the passenger side of the car.

I have no idea how I got on the other side of the station wagon. It truly was a miracle.

I remember no other sensory feedback, except the vibration in my hands. No light, sounds; nothing.

What happened? Obviously, it was a miracle, but I don't recall anything else out of the ordinary with the incident. I didn't feel a presence, nor did anything else happen to my car or to the station wagon. I was just suddenly on the other side.

Praise God.

THE CATCH

This is the testimony of Dan Cassidy. In the early 1970's, during the energy shortage, I was working on a small country cottage installing blown-in insulation. The A-frame ladder that I was using was six or eight feet tall. I was standing on the top step; the one that's always marked, *"Not a step."* Yes, that one.

The ground gave way under the right side of the ladder. As I looked down, it looked like the ground just disappeared from under that leg. Suddenly, I was falling to the right, head first, toward the ground. I fell so fast that my arms were waving at my sides. I had no time to protect my head and neck. Before I could hit the ground, my co-worker, Bill, reached out and caught me by the leg around my ankle.

I could feel my hair passing through the grass as he held me swinging in the air. I was that close to a broken neck. Bill then lowered me down gently.

During this time of my life, I weighed 140 to 150 pounds, plus the extra mass gained through acceleration in the fall. My head had travelled 12 to 14 feet; the combination of my height and the ladder. The Lord placed my co-worker in the exact right place, had him react instantly, and gave him the strength to hold me, and break my fall completely using only one hand. Thanks, and glory to the Lord for saving my life.

THE LADY WITH THE ROSARY TATOO

While passing by a local watering hole in southern Ohio, I became terribly famished, and I wanted to eat some fish and chips. This was strange since I had just eaten 15 minutes before. I knew this was our Lord telling me to go into this bar, because He had something in mind. The Lord had brought me to a very interesting lady named Martha. As she came down the bar, I knew I was there to meet with her, for on her way she passed by many younger and more attractive men than myself to sit just one stool away on my right.

As we sat, I noticed that she had a rosary tattooed down her whole left arm and hand. So, I asked her why she had a faith-based tattoo. She told me that while driving a sports car at 130 miles per hour, she lost control, and the car rolled and rolled, and was completely destroyed. She, on the other hand, was completely unharmed.

Knowing her life had been saved by His mighty hand, she had the rosary tattooed on her arm. She wanted a constant reminder of what He had done for her.

We talked for a while, and I told her a little about what God has done for me. She then told me that she had been having a rough time of late and needed a break. I reminded her of His great love and how He had saved her life, and that He would see her through.

I walked her home. She lived just a few houses from where I was parked.

When I returned to the bar, there was another young lady there whom He also wanted me to talk to. She was dancing an Irish jig; very well, I would say, so I watched for several minutes. She was there hoping to meet a future husband, so it became my job and pleasure to tell her that she was simply in the wrong place. She just needed to move down the street, to a place with a less lost crowd. This bar was a very rough place indeed.

It is my hope that if our Lord wants me to go into another place like this, that they serve better food. The fish and chips left something to be desired.

GOD'S SUPERNATURAL INTERVENTION

This is the testimony of Marty Younger.

DROWNING: There are two ways of having to leave this life that I felt I would never want to experience. I never would have dreamed that I would have one of them happen to me. I am referring to drowning and fire. I trust I will never have to share my testimony of the 2nd one, but I do have a personal experience of what it feels like to drown.

In Oklahoma we have an unusual way to catch fish when you do not have a pole or bait. It is called "Noodling". That is where you get in the river and reach down to where the fish are and catch it using your bare hands.

A couple of my high school buddies and I were at the Virgin Dam in Blackwell, Oklahoma when my drowning happened. Of course, it wasn't planned by any means, and little did I know that it would happen that day.

The best time to catch fish with your bare hands is during a time when the river is rising, and the location where we were noodling is just below a Dam. The fish seem to congregate there as the water rises and becomes deeper. However, it also becomes very rapid, and currents can change extremely fast. The noise level is so loud that you can't hear a person right next to you. We were spread out about ten to 15 feet apart.

I remember the river coming over the dam was getting stronger and swifter as the water continued to rise. It was getting hard to keep our balance, but we kept trying to get that *one* big catch. Suddenly, my feet slipped out from under me and I found my head going under the water, and my feet being shot up to the surface. It just flipped me upside down. I began to struggle, trying to get myself up right so I could stand up, but the water was just too swift, and was getting deeper. I struggled and fought with all I could to get turned around, but my air was running out fast.

At this point, I had fought until I could not hold my breath any longer. I said to myself, *"Well, here goes,"* and with that, I let my air out and sucked in water, trying to breathe. The last thing I remember before I passed out was saying to myself, *"Well, this isn't such a bad way to go."* As far as I knew, I had drowned.

The next thing that happened was what I do call a miracle. It was as if a hand was holding my head up out of the water, and I was vomiting up water out of my lungs. As I regained consciousness, I found myself several yards downstream from where I was noodling, and the guys were still up there, unaware that anything had happened to me.

All I can think of is when I passed out, my body quit fighting the current and I relaxed, so the river was able to spit me out, so to speak. The thing I can't explain, and will never forget, is how when I became conscious, I could feel that invisible hand holding my head above the water until I was able to stand up again.

PROTECTING BUBBLE

While in Arkansas, the Lord had my wife, her sister, and I meet another person who He had saved from serious injury and death. Sharon and I were in a swimming pool with a missionary family that we had just met. Their children were singing their favorite worship songs. I noticed another lady, Pam, enjoying the children's praising of the Lord. She didn't say anything at that time not wanting to change the moment. Yet somehow, I knew we would see each other again for she had something to tell me.

Later that day I met Pam again, and she offered this testimony. While she was riding on the interstate in St. Louis, she, along with her friend, were involved in a violent crash. The accident caused so much damage to their car that it was shown on the local news.

Just before impact, she and her friend felt a protective bubble form around them, something like the force fields of science fiction. While they both suffered some minor injuries – cuts to her left arm, caused by broken glass – the condition of the car was scrap. She told me they would have died, if not for the Lord's shield.

EACH DAY IS A GIFT

Sometime during the 1980's, I saw a newspaper article about a car accident in Rochester, New York. The picture showed a ball of metal that used to be a vehicle. It was crumpled like a ball of aluminum foil, and had a head sticking out of the top of the wreckage. The body was painstakingly cut from the metal, and the victim walked away with only minor injuries. That picture spoke volumes, and I carried it in my wallet for over 15 years. Eventually, it became so worn and faded that the mental image was clearer than the newspaper picture. I could write pages about that picture, but I will let you form the mental image and ponder it yourself.

I've experienced a series of events during my lifetime that have made me realize that our physical life is only a part of our existence. That death is not final, and that while we have choice, we are not in control. Sometimes God protects us from the perils of life, and sometimes God gives us the strength, or the patience, or the faith to survive. I could write several chapters about these various events, and they might interest or inspire, but today I am only moved to write about the two latest and largest of them.

In 2013, I was diagnosed with Non-Hodgkin lymphoma (large diffuse B for those of you well versed on the variations). It's very aggressive but quite treatable, and the outcomes are frequently good. I, however, was already at stage four, and three quarters of my bone marrow was already cancerous. It was obvious that my oncologist hoped to extend my life a little, but was not expecting a good outcome. I had a chemo port surgically implanted and began a series of 17 weeks of some serious chemotherapy. One of the chemicals was only a few ccs, but had to be injected slowly over several minutes so it wouldn't stop my heart. Many people prayed for me, but I can honestly say that I didn't. I was surprisingly comfortable with my fate, and chose to enjoy each day as a gift.

After the first treatment, my tumors shrunk by half. A PET scan after the second treatment showed the tumors to be gone. The oncologist recommended continuing with four more treatments as planned. The chemicals were known to have some nasty side effects, but I never experienced any of them. I lost my hair but never lost my lunch.

Four months after my confirmed diagnosis, my PET scan and a bone marrow biopsy showed no detectable traces of cancer. Three and a half years later, I am still here and still cancer free.

I don't know why I survived cancer and so many others do not. My doctors did not expect me to still be here. I can tell you that it's not because I deserve to be. I can tell you that I personally knew kinder, sweeter, better people who did not survive. I'm not in church every Sunday, and I'm not here to tell you how God heals or what God wants you to do with your life. All I can tell you is that each day is a gift. You can enjoy it, or you can worry about it: it's your choice. You may have strength, or wisdom, or knowledge that enable you to change your day. You may have faith that enables you to believe things will work out, even though you can't change them. You may have the serenity to accept things when they do not work out. All of these are gifts also, and if you are given them, you should use them. Just enjoy your gifts and accept that God is in charge. You may disagree, but I can tell you that *we* are not in charge.

If this story was not strong enough to make you ponder, let me continue with another. I don't have a picture for you to carry in your wallet like the car accident photo I used to carry, but I do have a story just as phenomenal.

I had been riding motorcycles with the Patriot Guard before my cancer diagnosis. I had been on a dozen or so missions with them, escorting funerals for veterans and first responders. I continued to ride with them after my treatments, until March of 2015. I was returning home from a wake on my motorcycle when I was struck from behind by a careless driver.

I was on a familiar road cruising along at 55 to 60 in a 55 mile per hour zone, when I crested the top of a hill with a stop light and a four-way intersection at the bottom. Traffic was stopped, and I braked a little harder than normal, and slowed to about 15 to 20 miles per hour as I approached the stopped cars. I could see the light was green, and wondered why traffic was still stopped. I swung out toward the center line, so I could see the cars ahead, and noted the lead car not moving yet, but not signaling a left turn either. I heard a noise coming from behind me. Before I could identify it or look in the mirror, I felt the bike ripped out from under me and I was in the air dropping to the pavement. I rolled a few times, realizing I had been hit from behind.

As I rolled, I then realized something large was coming at me fast. I was hit square in the back by the cars' bumper and violently propelled forward again. As I continued to roll, I became cognizant that the car was gaining on me again.

I was then looking up at the underside of the car right in front of my eyes, with the left front tire coming at my head. At that point, I knew my number had come up, but then I was surprised to find myself airborne, several feet off the ground. As the pavement approached, I somehow resisted the urge to reach out, and just tucked my arms in and rolled some more. As I rolled to a stop, I realized I had survived, at least for the moment.

I noticed that people were gathering at the road side. I could see my motorcycle laying in the road to my left. It had apparently rolled alongside me. I heard gasps of surprise as I sat up and looked over at it. *"He is sitting up."* I realized my back hurt and lay back down. When the ambulance arrived, the emergency responders were surprised to find me conscious and aware. They said I had been thrown over 300 feet from the impact. The driver claimed to have been doing 55 mph, though I suspect she was going faster. The police report said she hit me 25 feet into her skid. I guess that was the initial brief noise that I couldn't identify. A witness at the scene spoke to me and said he saw her tire hit my helmet.

Because of the violence of the accident, they wanted to airlift me to a trauma center, but since I was conscious, and they could see no severe injury, it was my choice. I chose to be taken by ambulance to a local hospital. When I arrived, they were prepping for potential surgery on a 67-year-old male who had been thrown over 300 feet by a car. They were a little confused when I got there, and they were presented with a 67-year-old male with multiple abrasions.

They took x-rays and cleaned my abrasions. I walked out of the emergency room later with no stitches, no broken bones, no internal bleeding, and a very sore back. The x-rays showed a compression fracture in the lower vertebrae of my back. They seemed to doubt the x-rays, because I wasn't complaining of severe pain and was able to sit without assistance. A back specialist doubted the diagnosis the following week because I was improving so rapidly.

As I mentioned earlier, I don't have a picture for you to carry in your wallet like the car accident clipping I used to carry. I do have a story just as phenomenal. I was hit by a car at high speed and propelled the length of a football field, and survived (basically without injury). The back injury they did diagnose was doubted because I recovered too fast. Spin that any way you want, it's still incredible.

My story doesn't end there. What is even more incredible than my physical survival is my mental survival. As I lay there on the side of the road, I heard *"I'm so sorry, I'm so sorry."* I could see a young brunette woman out of the corner of my right eye. She almost killed me, but I didn't feel angry. I guess that would have been understandable. I just felt okay. I guess this would be a better story if I said I looked her way and told her it was okay or something comforting, but I just didn't feel the need to relieve her pain.

Friends urged me to get a lawyer and seek a settlement. TV ads for ambulance chasing lawyers assure me they can get me tons of money. When I tell friends it's not about money, they tell me stories of people who were not punished with lawsuits and went on to hurt someone else.

How would I feel if she kills the next motorcycle rider? Once or twice I have almost succumbed to that logic. Then wonder how I will feel, knowing I have once again been given the gift of another day, but used it to profit or to punish?

Once again, I don't know why I survived without injury while others die from lesser impacts. I've stopped wondering. Death will come to all, but it will come in His time, and in His way. If I am wrong, and life is nothing but a string of coincidences leading to a random conclusion, there is still nothing to be gained by struggling against things that are not within your control. There is everything to be gained by looking at each day as a gift, and listening to that still small voice when it prompts you to do something.

ROCKY'S ROAD

Twenty years ago, I was on my way to Mississippi, via the interstate. I was delivering a truck load of USA Today Newspapers. I was driving my little gray Nissan while listening to Kenneth Copeland. I had made it as far as Theodore, Alabama, on this very foggy early morning.

I was following a large truck very closely when the trucker turned on his flashers, as he was slowing down. I started to pass around him, but as soon as I did, I saw lights right in front of me. I froze, so close were the lights. A white van was traveling the wrong way on the interstate. Then I found myself behind the truck once again. I had done nothing, as I stated before: I froze.

I stopped at a store in Pascagoula, Mississippi. As I was talking to the store clerk, telling of how my life had just been saved, a man walked up and identified himself as the driver of the truck. He asked me how I did it. I told him I didn't; *God did.*

THE ANGEL'S PROTECTION

YOU SHOULD BE DEAD! Some people believe that life is full of coincidences. Especially those times that we would call "a close call". I personally believe that God, in his rich mercy, intervenes during those times. One such example is the following testimony.

While I was attending Bible School in Waxahachie, Texas, I had gotten a job at the Joy Manufacturing Plant which for a full-time student was an excellent job, and hard to get. Of course, one reason is that they would have to invest in training you to operate their machinery.

I had finally gotten promoted to a powerful machine that would cut still parts and make bolts, nuts, anything on the tool side of equipment. This machine would spin very fast to cut out these parts. It was called a Turret Lathe.

During training, the supervisor was showing me how to handle the lathe. It had a rapid run forward gear on it, so you could run it quicker up to the part you were going to cut into. He warned me to be careful not to get too close to the part. Only close enough to hand move the lathe up to the part being worked on. There was another, heavier part, that would hold smaller steel rods, so you could make smaller bolts. This thing weighed about 25 pounds or so, and was secured by steel chunks. The motor would spin these parts at a rapid rate of speed.

I had it going about 1000 revolutions per minute as he was showing me how to bring up the lathe. I reached over and pulled the rapid forward gear and said, *"Like this?"*

It shot forward and hit the 25-pound part, and broke the jaws. The 25-pound part flew out of the machine at blinding speed, right toward my face. It stopped in midair, and dropped down to our feet. The Supervisor, with a pale look, said stuttering, *"y-you should-d-d be dead!"* Without thinking, I said, *"The Angel of the Lord encamps about those who fear him!"*

It truly was a miracle that my boss could not explain, but I will forever be grateful for my angel protecting me that day from death!

OVER TURNED TRUCK

One day I was in my truck. The truck was loaded with round bales of hay. Not those small ones popular in the Eastern US, but the truly gigantic bales used in the western states. My truck overturned. While the truck rolled, time seemed to stop, and every detail became very vivid. I heard a voice say, *"Move to the other side of the truck."* I slid across the seat to the other side of the cab.

Immediately, one of the large bales struck the cab, crushing the roof down to the steering wheel. If I had not moved, I would have been crushed. I then experienced a sense of peace and safety that I had never felt before.

PEDAL TO THE METAL

God saves me once again, by Dan Cassidy.

In the early 1970's, on a perfect day with clear skies and dry roads, and with an excuse to drive too fast. Not that I needed one, but it was nice to have one. Cars in that period had distributors and points. If you drove as my uncle did, like a little old lady, the spark plugs would become fouled, causing the engine to run rough. So, my uncle gave me his 1965 tan F85 Oldsmobile Cutlass to clean the plugs. This was done by driving it as hard and fast as I could make it go.

With the pedal to the metal, I was doing 90 to 100 miles per hour. I was heading west when a car with a man and woman heading south pulled out only 30 to 40 feet in front of me. There was not enough time or distance to stop or to turn. I had a momentary blackout that felt like I did not exist for a split second. I then found myself heading north on the road they pulled out from with my speed reduced to 5 to 10 miles per hour.

At the time this occurred, I tried to convince myself that there must be a rational explanation for what had just happened. I convinced myself that I must have hit the brakes hard, turned hard to the right, and spun *just right*. The tires must have gained traction at just the right moment to propel me down the side road. The blackout was caused by panic. Man, what a great driver I am.

Even then, I knew that this explanation couldn't hold water. This car did not have anti-lock brakes. Braking that hard would have locked the tires, filling the air with noise and the smell of burning rubber. There was no sound. In fact, I probably never reached for the brake pedal. Turning 90 degrees at that speed and distance, would certainly defy some natural laws of physics.

I looked in my rearview mirror, expecting to see two terrified people. Instead, I saw a man and woman laughing and having a good time. They were only half way through their turn. I believe they never saw my car on either road. Why they did not see me, I don't know.

They do not know, that which I do now. On this day, God saved all of our lives, either by moving my car thru time and space, or having it do a Bat-Turn (circa the old *Batman* TV show). To God alone goes the glory and my thanks.

HAND OF GOD

Thank God! He never grows weary; this is saved number three for me, Dan Cassidy, number four you have already read. See also *God goes to church*.

While working on a very extensive project that had been ongoing for a couple of years, installing mastic and granules, and painting window framing on a concrete building; the old *Selby Shoe Company*, built probably in the 1920's. This building covered a city block and was four or five stories high. In Portsmouth, Ohio, there is a mural of this building on their flood wall if you happen to see it.

We were using a swing stage: a device often used by window washers on high rise buildings. Our rig on this job consisted of a 24-foot aluminum platform, suspended by electric drill cable climbers at each end. Two steel beams supported and suspended the cables, with two moveable carts, and 36 cinder blocks acting as a counterweight, all tied together with cables and clamps.

Since the cables and clamps were the heart of the system, a failure of the clamps and cables would cause a system failure and a nasty fall. We would check this system at the beginning of the day, at lunch, at the end of the day, and at any time we moved the stage.

Throughout the months we worked on this project, never were the clamps even slightly loose, until one most *unusual day*. We had finished that day's drop and went up to move the rig for the next day's work, something we had done many times. On this day, however, the clamps were completely loose on the side I was going to move.

Looking at the loose cables lying there, I thought *"What happened to the clamps?"* Then I looked again and couldn't believe what I was seeing: the cables were not clamped to the cinder blocks, they were just lying there. What could have been holding us up? Looking at the loose cables, I thought they must have become jammed, and that is what must have happened, but there wasn't anything for the cables to become attached to. The carts were constructed with round tubing, allowing free movement of the cables.

I know now what I couldn't even believe then. We had checked the system at lunch 4 hours previous, and all was fine. Somehow, for possibly 4 hours, we had just hung on the side of a building, held in the air by nothing physical. There would not have been time (the time it would take for us to take an elevator to the roof) from the ground for someone to loosen the bolts before we reached the roof, nor would anyone have reason to, to my knowledge,

I never mentioned the loose cables to my co-worker, but have often wondered in later years if his were loose as well. I don't know who or what loosened the cables, but I do know that we were held in the air by the Hand of God.

Decades after this event I met a prophet, who told me that the Lord had saved my life six times. This was surely one of those times. Why He saved me so many times, I do not know. Perhaps so I could tell you of this most unusual afternoon.

He replied, "You of little faith, why are you so afraid?" Then he got up and rebuked the winds and the waves, and it was completely calm. **Matthew 8:26**

Chapter Five

Returned From The Other Side

Then he went up and touched the coffin, and those carrying it stood still. He said, "Young man, I say to you, get up!" The dead man sat up and began to talk, and Jesus gave him back to his mother. **Luke 7:14-15**

ADDICT SENT BACK

A man I met in a restaurant told me about his son. His son had a drug addiction, and had overdosed near a first responder building. When they arrived to help him, he had already turned blue, and stayed that way as they worked on him for six more minutes. When he regained consciousness, he said, *"I did not see God, but I heard Him say 'I do not want you to die in this manner, so go back.'"* Back he came, free of his addiction.

A FOGGY MORNING

More than half a century ago, Judy was driving to work on a foggy morning. She failed to see a garbage truck stopped on the road while its driver was picking up trash. This was before the trucks were fitted with the flashing safety lights in use today. Judy drove her Volkswagen Beetle under the truck. At the hospital, her family was told that *she would not make it.*

She told me that in fact they were in fact right. She would die twice in the weeks before she left the hospital. The first time she died, she saw a bright light in the distance, and as she approached it, she was met by her old Baptist minister, who told her to *go back.*

Her injuries were severe, and she would fade in and out of consciousness, and she died a second time. The second time, she drew even closer to the light. She was then met a second time by her minister, who told her the Lord wanted her to go back, and to give her testimony to all who would listen. This she has faithfully done for the past 55 years. That is how Judy came to give us this testimony while having coffee at a McDonalds.

SPEAKING TO JESUS

My preference has always been for the person sharing the testimony to also write it. This ensures more details and greater accuracy. This is especially true of this testimony, given to us by a lady in Alabama. This is a testimony given to her upon her mother's return from heaven, including a conversation that her mother had with Jesus.

Her testimony is so unique, and in spite of my own misgivings, I have decided to include it. I believe readers have a right to hear it.

Her mother died! Upon her death, she went to heaven. There she spent some time talking to Jesus. While they were conversing, Jesus said *"You have been dead for some time now. You can stay, or you can go back, the choice is yours."* She replied *"I would like to stay, but what do you want me to do?"* He said *"I would like you to return, so that people will know that I am real."*

Dan's notation:

Please forgive my lack of detail; how she died, of what, how long she was dead. I was so certain that this lady would give us her written account that I did not ask her questions or make notes of her testimony.

IN THE FOOTSTEPS OF ELIJAH

This is the testimony of a missionary, on one of his many trips to Central and South America. His mission is and was to serve the poor in this region. On this trip, he was serving in Ecuador. The Lord God was in attendance and ten thousand people were there also. Some of the people had walked for days to be there.

He had purchased two thousand chickens to distribute, not enough for a crowd of this size, but God multiplied them, and every family received a chicken.

In this group of believers there were many sufferings from various ailments, some who had suffered for years, and there were many healings. A lady then came to this man of God with her deceased six-year-old child. Acting on faith and the guidance of the Holy Spirit, he took the boy and repeated the actions of Elijah when he prayed for the widow's son.

Then he stretched himself out on the boy three times and cried out to the Lord, "O Lord my God, let this boy's life return to him!" The Lord heard Elijah's cry and the boy's life returned to him, and he lived. ***1 Kings 17: 21-22***

The Lord also heard the missionary, and the boy's life returned to him, and he returned the child to his mother.

GOD ANSWERS PRAYER

In March of 2011, my husband and I were working at *Juniper Springs Campground* in Silver Springs, Florida. We were both working a standard forty-hour week, until the first of July of the same year. My husband had gone to the doctors in Astor, Florida. After doing a EKG and blood work, they discovered his hemoglobin level had dropped to 5.5 grams per deciliter of blood. The normal range for a healthy man is 14-18 gm/dL They admitted him to Monroe Regional Hospital in Ocala, Florida, where they gave him six units of blood. The doctors said it was a wonder he had not dropped dead working so many hours.

After further tests, they concluded that he had colon cancer. In mid-July of 2011, he started six weeks of chemo and radiation therapy, going five days a week. He wore a chemo pump, and once a week he would go to get his pump filled. He would then be good to go for another week, but he also underwent radiation therapy five days a week. With about 100 miles of traveling every day. He did very well, no side effects or anything from either of the treatments. Thank you, Lord.

Later that year, on a Saturday morning in early October, I was collecting what I needed for work that morning, when *something* told me to return to our camper, which I did. As I walked in, our little dog was on the couch, licking where he had been sitting. I walked over and pulled the towel back. It was full of blood. I then looked in the bathroom and found my husband unconscious. I thought he was dead. He had already started to turn blue. I started screaming for help. Our co-workers came running over and asked if I had called emergency services. I said no. It just so happened that an ambulance was close by, which came and got him, taking him to the hospital, which was 50 miles away.

At the hospital, they said that he didn't have a drop of his own blood left inside him. You tell me that the hand of God spared my husband's life for a reason, that day before my birthday on October 9th. That Sunday morning was my birthday and I kept praying *Lord don't let nothing happen to my husband on my birthday because if you do, you might as well take me with him*. I walked to the hospital, and after taking one look at him, said *thank you Lord for sparing his life*. He had his color back, and was walking around the hall, as if nothing had happened.

He underwent his first surgery on October 10th, and two weeks later he had a blockage in his stomach, for which they had to open him up again. Thank you Lord; my husband has been cancer free for five years now. To God goes the glory. My husband is a walking testimony to Gods healing power.

Dan's notation:

This lady's husband would later tell me that throughout this ordeal he felt some unseen hand holding his own.

When he had said this, Jesus called in a loud voice, "Lazarus, come out!" The dead man came out, his hands and feet wrapped with strips of linen, and a cloth around his face. Jesus said to them, "Take off the grave clothes and let him go." John 11:43-44

Chapter Six

Other Blessings

"If that is how God clothes the grass of the field, which is here today and tomorrow is thrown into the fire, will he not much more clothe you, O you of little faith?" **Matthew 6:30**

WHO NEEDS THE MAYTAG REPAIRMAN?

While I was a single mom on a very restricted budget, our washer died. With no money to replace it, I prayed that it would begin working again. Without a washer for a couple of weeks, I walked by it one day and I said another prayer. The washer began working. That washer continued to work for many years.

HELPING HAND PLUMBING

The water pipe to our house broke. Of course, it was on the side of the house that I was responsible for. I had no idea how to repair a leak, but began by digging up the most saturated part of the yard. I became very frustrated and called a plumber. When he arrived, I watched every move he made! I observed how to identify the leak, measure the length of the needed parts, and how to repair the leak. Just in case, I even saved the parts that he removed.

I later had a second leak. This time, I took matters into my own hands. After many hours, I repaired the leak myself, mad as could be at the situation. I let God know how angry I was at Him for letting it happen again. Approximately three weeks later, I found myself repairing another leak myself. I dug industriously for what seemed an eternity. I cried, and finally prayed for help. I went into town to get parts. I was a muddy mess, and I had been crying and praying on my way into town that it would never happen again.

Once home, I began to bail water that had filled the hole. Suddenly, a small group of boys were in my yard. I had never seen them before. They offered to fix the leak, and they did. That was the last leak I had.

WHICH WAY DO I GO?

On a trip to Florida, the Lord blessed me with a visit to Sebastian, a small community on the central-Atlantic side of the state. The Lord lead me to many fellow Christians, and to a young non-Christian couple who had moved there from Nepal. As we talked, the conversation turned to God: both mine and theirs. When I told them about our God, they were receptive to the message. When I had to leave, I asked them to promise me that they would – that night – ask the true God to reveal Himself to them. They promised that they would.

I then left the beach area, preparing for my departure. Upon reaching the parking lot, I had and still have a feeling that there was something that I should do in this area of Florida. I had promised my wife and friends that I would be back in time for church on Sunday. To keep my word, I needed to leave immediately.

Confused as to the way to go, I said a prayer *asking for direction*. I am not sure if I had finished the prayer when one of my new friends came around the corner with my answer. He said that he lived in Melbourne, and that Melbourne is a beautiful city, and that I should visit Melbourne. I thanked him, and told him that he was the vessel that my God had used to answer my prayer. I told him that he had said the name of his town three times in one sentence. I told him I was just praying for direction, and explained why.

For you see, for me to go home from where we were, I would pass through Melbourne. To God be the glory. Thanks to His direction, I made it to church on time, *and* my young friend got to witness the power of our Lord to answer prayer.

A PIECE OF PIE

A few years back, I volunteered through my workplace, to help in preparing and serving a Thanksgiving luncheon for those less fortunate. It was a very humbling experience, as many men, women and children slowly proceeded down the buffet line for a meal that I took for granted every year. It was the typical menu of roast turkey, dressing, mashed potatoes, and three or four types of pies for desert, one of which was pecan, my all-time favorite! I remember mentioning jokingly to a fellow volunteer that I hoped a piece would be left for me after the guests were served.

After the cafeteria was cleaned up and the food put away, I looked around to make sure that nothing had been missed, and there on the counter where the various pies were served, was exactly one piece of pie left, and to my disbelief and delight, it was pecan. I did feel kind of sheepish to proceed and eat it, so I casually asked if anyone minded if I ate it, which no one did.

It was the best piece of pecan pie that I had eaten in a while. I have recounted this to many friends and relatives. I firmly believe this was no coincidence and will always consider it a *thank you* from God for my services that day. I still participate in this Thanksgiving Day luncheon. Not expecting a remaining piece of pecan pie, but the good feeling that comes from helping others.

A SPECIAL BLESSING FOR ME

Cincinnati, like most American towns, has special events to help the poor during the holiday season. A few years back my wife and I had the opportunity to serve two consecutive years. This event is a huge undertaking, with hundreds of volunteers, and many sponsors. People are fed, given health care, necessary supplies, clothes, and even transportation. The organizers do their best to meet everyone's needs as much as possible in a one-day event.

My wife served meals one year, and did face painting the next. I worked giving out coats both years. The coats were passed out on the second floor, with escalators at both ends of a huge hallway. The coats were on racks arranged by size and gender.

The volunteers would meet the customers at the top of the escalators, then escort them to the coat racks to help them select their coat. Several hours into the event, during my first year working this event, I met a woman at the escalator and she said to me, *"I know that God has a special blessing for me."* As we walked, we talked about God, as she is a street preacher. On our way to the smaller ladies' coats, she explained, *"I am looking for a full-length black fur coat like the coats women wore in the past."* I had been there several hours and had not seen a coat like she wanted. I was sure she would be disappointed. When we reached the coats, there it was: a black full-length fur coat, hanging on the end of the rack. She tried it on and it looked as if it had been tailor-made for her. A perfect fit, a special blessing.

The next year, as I was telling two young female volunteers about this lady and her coat, she came up behind me, and said my name, and that this year she wanted a brown fur coat. She then reached out and picked up *her* coat hanging on the end of the rack. Again, it was a perfect fit. Then she walked away, while the two girls and I looked on in amazement.

The coats that are given away are mostly lightly used, but a few are purchased new for this event. Coats for very large men are often in short supply, and are specifically purchased. I had just helped a man find one of these coats, and when he put it on, it fit. I was happy to have been a help to him. Then he saw another large man looking for a coat, a man he didn't know. He removed his coat and gave it to the stranger, saying *this coat would look good on you.* This is one of the most unselfish acts I have ever witnessed. He had so little, yet he gave away possibly the most valuable and needed thing he had.

There were no more extra-large coats on the customer's racks, so I went to the storage area in the back and asked if there were any left. The lady said there were none. I told her what had happened, and she decided to look again. She came back with a coat identical with the first and I took it to the most generous man I have ever met.

BAPTISM

The church we attend believes in full immersion baptism. I was baptized as a child and believed that this baptism covered the required baptism. My husband was also baptized as a child and believed the same. We were convicted of this belief. One weekend, when I was visiting my sister, I received a deep calling that I needed to be baptized publicly, by immersion, at our church.

When we arrived home – myself, from Missouri, and my husband from Kentucky – and we reviewed our weekends, he also had come to the same conclusion, at approximately the same time as I had. We were baptized together, in our church, by immersion, the very next weekend.

FORGIVENESS

While stopping for something to eat, on a trip to Florida, I met a young man named Kevin, from Georgia. He was a small man, 130 to 140 pounds, tops. His father and brother are both larger, and are both violent men. They would often beat him up. On one occasion, his brother hurt him so severely that he needed emergency surgery to repair his spleen. His doctor told him that the operation was very high risk, and that he could possibly die in surgery. Before he would consent to the surgery, he requested to see his father and brother. When he spoke to them, he told them that he forgave them, for what they had done to him, following the example set by the Lord. Did I say that he was a small man? I was wrong he is a very big man.

IDOL BURNING MOM

My mother was born in Japan. She emigrated to the United States, where she accepted Jesus. Upon returning home to Japan, she entered our family home. She then gathered up all the family idols took them out into the garden and set them on fire. Her family disowned her, and she returned to the United States.

MIRACLE GIRL

Sometime between March 8th and March 13th in 2015, the Lord blessed me by having me meet one of His living miracles. She was a young child three or four years old. I encountered her at the *Wyndham Cypress Palm Resort* in Kissimmee, Florida, while I was crossing a parking lot. She was a beautiful blonde girl who just glowed with the

Spirit of God. I was immediately drawn to her. She was accompanied by her mother, and, I believe, her grandmother. When they introduced me, they said, *"She is our miracle child."*

Her mother told me that when she was pregnant, the doctors told her that the fetus had so many medical problems that she should seek an abortion. Her mother, a person of great faith, said *"No. She is my daughter, a gift from God, and I will love and care for her, no matter what."* I do not know what medical treatments that she may have had, or may need in the future, but standing before me was what seemed to be a completely healthy young girl, with a great big smile, and a spirit that delighted me just to be near her.

After we talked for a while, I had to leave, so I turned to go back to my room. Having walked away about twenty to twenty-five feet, I turned back, and she blew me a kiss. That was over two years ago I am still touched by her innocent act of love.

The day after this, my friend and I were to meet His prophet. The prophet told me some of my past, and some events in my future. If the Lord said that I could only meet one or the other – the prophet Nathan, or the miracle girl – I believe that I would choose her, so powerful was her effect on me. I give thanks to the Lord that her mother did not listen to the doctors. If you are ever blessed by meeting her, you will too.

GIFT OF A ROSARY

A good friend of mine – she's someone I think more of as a daughter than a friend – Lori and I were talking about God. I was kidding her about putting on my dancing shoes. I had repeatedly told her that I want to dance with her at her wedding. She is seeing a young man, and I reminded her that God likes it when we marry. I told her that God can give you blessings when you do. She knows that whenever I bring up my dancing shoes, I am really asking her about her wedding plans.

On this day, her son, Charlie, was with her at the donut store where she works. We started talking about marriage, and God's desire for her to wed. Then Charlie walked up and said, *"I love talking about God!"* Lori and I looked at each other, and said at the same time, *"Father Charlie."* Charlie was 12 years old, if I remember his age correctly.

God walks ahead of us, sometimes years ahead. Decades ago, in a dark period of my life, I went to see Father Patterson. I knew him to be a fine man and a great priest. When I told him that I was separating from my wife, and how I had brought this on myself, we talked a while. He then did a most unusual thing. He reached into his pocket and gave me his personal rosary. I thanked him and left.

I took the rosary with me and kept it many years. Many times, I would be tempted to throw it away, when it would show up in a drawer or a box of things. I could not let it go until after that day in the donut shop. It had reappeared in a drawer full of stuff just a couple days before.

I knew as soon as we said, *"Father Charlie"* that Father Patterson had not given the rosary to me. I was only to keep it for Charlie. I gave it to Lori a couple of days later, with a note to give it to Charlie when she felt the time was right. To God alone goes the glory for this short testimony, 30 years in the making.

SOMETHING CRAZY

I am 15 years old. Last summer, I went to an outdoor multi-day Christian concert. It was my friend's idea. It was also his idea that we do *"something crazy"* for the concert. So, we took t-shirts and wrote in big letters *"Free Hugs"* on the front. On the back, we wrote *"Free Prayers."*

Lots of people came to us for the free hugs, telling us what a cool idea it was and how good it felt to be hugged. We were enjoying the concert, but I couldn't help feeling that I, just a teenage boy, was making a difference, however small. It wasn't hard to give out hugs, and to be honest getting reciprocal hugs felt really good too. I remember thinking how happy I was that my friend had his *"crazy"* idea.

About 30 minutes after the concert started, a woman came up to me. She was crying. She told me about how her husband said he was a Christian but, in her opinion, he wasn't living a life that reflected that. Then she told me that her son seemed to be falling away from his faith. He was supposed to come with her that night, but when the day came, he refused. The woman began crying harder and told me that she was afraid for them, and how that crushed her heart. She had been praying for them, but she was very discouraged. She asked me to pray for her, so, I did. I don't have a clue what I said, but since I am very talkative, I bet it was a long prayer. By the end, I could feel the woman resting her body against mine. Without saying a word, she gave me a wonderful hug and walked away. I could tell she was still sad and thought about how not all prayers are answered right away, some not in the way we want, and some not at all. I hoped God heard my prayer.

My friend and I walked around the crowd for a while. We saw a group of people that had "Free Hugs" written on their bodies. Some had painted "Free Hugs" on their foreheads, cheeks, and arms. They were giving out lots of hugs. They talked with us for a little while, then we started walking around again.

I felt a tap on my shoulder. It was the woman who was afraid for her husband and son. She was so happy to see me. She told me that she had just received a phone call from her husband. She shook her phone near my chest as if she wanted to prove he had called. Her husband had told her that he and their son were coming to the concert. She kept thanking me for praying for her family. We praised God. We gave God all the praise.

I continue to praise God for being able to see Him at work as He was that night. I think I see more of God's work every day. I am more convinced that with God's help, I can impact the world. I hope someday I will help someone else make the decision to follow Jesus. Who knows?

ANNE'S YEARS OF SERVICE TO THE LORD

I was asked to drive a school bus for our local school of Williamsburg, Ohio, in September of 1974. I said yes, that I would give it a try. Our neighboring town of Bethel, Ohio, needed a late high school take home run, and they asked me to help them out.

My husband, Tom, was a plant maintenance engineer for *United Dairy Farmers* (U.D.F.) in Norwood, Ohio. We had five children, ages two to twelve, four girls and one boy.

Tom had been at U.D.F. for sixteen years, while concurrently attending Cincinnati Bible College. Early in the year of 1974, God began to speak to Tom about full-time ministry. We were ministering to several Nursing Homes, just on Sunday afternoons.

October of 1974 brought with it great struggles for Tom, challenging him to decide between being called to ministry in a full time capacity, or stay in his role at *United Dairy Farmers* until the children were raised.

One morning in October of 1974, I said to Tom, *"You have a choice to make. Stay on in your job, or go into ministry full time."* Three days later, Tom came home and announced that he had given U.D.F. his resignation. They accepted it, and God became our Provider in every way, and He never missed a beat. Food enough for seven people was always provided miraculously. We never missed a meal.

I bowed my head one night before going to sleep and asked God, *If He thought health care insurance for seven people was important and would He make a way.* Three days later, Bethel-Tate called and needed a full-time bus driver. The transportation director told me that it would provide our health insurance if we needed it. I worked full-time for two years, while our children attended Williamsburg local school. In the summer of 1976, after two years of driving the bus, I received a call from the Williamsburg's Superintendent, asking if I would be interested in a full-time position.

I have been a full-time bus driver for forty-two years, and forty of those forty-two has been with Williamsburg Local. Our five children are grown and raised, and we enjoy 16 grandchildren and seven great grandchildren.

We have *never* regretted our walking in faith. Our children, grandchildren, and great grandchildren all love the Lord and walk by faith. Forty-two years later, I am still driving a school bus and busy in nursing home ministry in the Ministry to the aged.

TO EVERLASTING RICHES - CAPTAIN OF MY SHIP

Life's journey has taken me to places, some can only dream of: fancy trucks, Escalades, vacations and my dream home. Being the CEO of a company, bringing in close to a million dollars a year. Well, as the dream manifested, I was humbled by the gifts that God had given me, thankful to live in such a manner as I had previously only dreamed of. I remember when I would get a new contract, or even a small personal achievement.

Each evening I would reflect on the day, kneeling at my king-size bed, thanking God for the gifts and blessings He had given me.

As the dream progressed, I began to not be thankful, but to be wrapped up in what so many chase for their whole lives: wealth, a nice home, a business, a relationship, material things. I had the new boat and the dream life with fancy trips, luxury cars, and was rubbing shoulders with multi-millionaires, and people from all walks of life.

I will never forget the day that changed so much. It was sunny, out with a boat full of people, as we cruised the Colorado lake. I was steering the ship and enjoying the sun on my face. I will never forget someone saying to me *wow, you have it all*.

As I smartly popped off *"I am the captain of this ship!"*

As of that moment, things in my life changed very quickly. Forgetting to humble myself and be thankful for my many blessings, my life did a 180 degree turn that I never imagined would happen.

I lost the house, the business, the fancy trips, the relationship I had worked so hard for, and yes, *even the boat*. It was all gone in less than a year, and in distress; emotionally, physically, and financially, I began to drink and became a very upset and angry person.

How could God have taken it all away, everything I had worked for my whole life. Everything that was gold and fancy, it was all gone or, so I thought. As I look back, I realize all the gifts that I was given, were given to me from God, as I only had a high school education, and excelled past what many family and friends thought I would accomplish. I realized that God had given me the fancy car, the nice home, and yes, even the boat. I realized at this moment in life that the day on the lake would be etched into my memory forever, never to be forgotten.

I am not the captain of my ship as I had claimed so proudly that fateful day. God was the Captain, and I was just a co-pilot holding on to the Pilot, who had guided me my whole life. God has taken me to places and shown me things in my life that only He could have provided, and yes, He also can take it all back in the blink of an eye, but God has shown me His gifts, and shown me His strength, as He still walks among us.

He is the Captain of my ship, and I thank Him daily for my many blessings.

HOME EARLY

One very cold and snowy day, I left work early. It was something out of the ordinary, since we had just built this house, and money was very tight. I don't know why, I just wanted to get home.

My wife and I both worked in town our while our first grader attended a rural school. When I arrived home some three hours early, I was shocked to find our son Bill standing in the snow at the corner of the garage. His school had let out early due to the weather, but they had not informed us. They just put him on a bus and dropped him off at our empty house. A house that we had moved into so recently we had not yet met any of our neighbors. The temperature was in the single digits and I shudder to think what could have happened if I had stayed at work that day.

TESTIMONIES FROM JERUSALEM

The Lord blessed me with a trip to Jerusalem for the *Feast of the Tabernacles* and the Blood Moon that occurred during the feast. While there, I stayed at the *Petra Hostel* in the Old City, and I was blessed to hear some testimonies from others who felt the need to be there at that time.

One of the ladies wanted to be there for the Blood Moon. She did her best to save for the trip, but still found herself short by a few hundred dollars. In the months before, her friend had told her that she should refinance her home to take advantage of the low interest rates. She did this to lower her monthly payment. She was unaware that monthly mortgage payment would not have to be made for the month of the refinance, and this provided her the money needed.

Another lady told me that she had only previously been in the Holy Land just a few weeks prior, yet felt she needed to return to see the Blood Moon. Having spent most of her savings on the previous visit, she too found herself a little short. She checked and rechecked the discount flights to try to find one in her budget. She was ready to give up when she heard His voice say, *"Try Again."* She did, and found a bargain deal that was short lived, booked her flight, and shared her testimony with us.

One of the men who came from Canada had recently awakened from slumber. He also felt a strong need to be in the Old City. His problem was a little different: he is in a mixed marriage. His wife is a Moslem. Their different faiths had not been a problem until his awakening. She could not understand the changes she saw in him. When he told her that he wished to go to Jerusalem, she said *not to use any of our money for your God*. He told a friend of his problem, to which his friend replied that he would love to help but could not afford to. Then his friend told one of his friends, and a friend of a friend provided the money. He then booked his room in the hostel on short notice, in a city that was over-booked due to the Feast.

A couple of the ladies from the hostel met a man who lived in Israel. This man was quite wealthy, and paid for a meal for quite a few of us, eight or nine if I recall correctly, all strangers to him. People he had only met in the last couple of days or, as was my case, a few minutes. He also said he would help one of the ladies that felt the need to stay in Israel, by finding her work and a place to stay.

After we finished eating, we were talking, just the two of us, and he shared his testimony. He was the oldest of six boys and his mother died while he was young. As the eldest, he felt it was his duty to care for his brothers. He prayed to God, and asked if God would give him the ability to make the money necessary to support his family. God then gave him more than was needed, and he understood that his wealth was a gift from God, so he loved to share it.

An interesting thing about this testimony is I had forgotten it, until the other day, some year and a half since I had heard it, I found my note in my car; a car I didn't own until recently. How it got there I have no idea. The simple fact that a two inch by four-inch piece of paper with 28 words on it followed me through two home moves, and a year of traveling the country in a RV. God must surly want someone to read this testimony.

ON THIS DAY ONE MAN TOOK ON THE SINS OF MEN AND DIED FOR OUR FORGIVENESS! A lady from China relayed this information to me to pass on. Two thousand years ago in China, a royal scribe to the emperor wrote these words into the official history.

MEETING A PROPHET

My meeting of the prophet was in the late evening. We were driving back to our hotel room in Orland, Florida. It had been a very long day and we were tired and hungry. Tom started giving directions to a restaurant. I thought he was listening to the GPS. He wasn't. He had turned it off. After many twists and turns, we arrived at a *Denny's* starved and totally lost. We sat down and ordered.

While we were eating, four people came in and passed by where we were sitting. When they were out of ear-shot, I remarked to Tom that for some reason, I felt I knew, or had some sort of connection to one of the ladies, even though we had never met. As their party reached their table, and as Rita started to sit, in a loud voice she said, *"Her name is Nelda, she is a Christian and is single!"* I responded that I too am Christian, but not single. I then went over to their table to give them some bookmarks for their bibles. I introduced myself to Rita, since we had already spoken. Rita then introduced me, first to Nelda, then Maria, (Nathan's wife) and finally Nathan. She said that Nathan is a prophet.

I asked Nathan if he had anything to tell me. He replied, *"It does not work that way."* I responded that I didn't know how it works, as I had never met a prophet before. I went over to his side of the table, and he touched me on my left side, with one finger, for a split second.

He then revealed to me three things that God had previously made known to me. First, that I had seen God (*God Goes to Church*). Second, that if I used my God given gifts wisely, my pay would be doubled (this occurred in July, 2016). Then he said that my son, William, and I would be reunited sometime in the future. I am waiting for this event. I do so miss him, and wonder how his life has been. Then God had Nathan tell me that He had saved my life six times. In a short time, I recalled five of them. Four of them are already in this book. The fifth one involved both myself and one other, and it has been my hope that she would give us her testimony for this book. Unfortunately, she has not, so I will give you the account from my perspective.

I was helping my brother insulate his home. As my brother fed the hopper with insulation, I would drill the holes, then fill them with the blown-in insulation. I was drilling the highest holes on the second floor, reaching out further than was safe, trying to get extra holes drilled without moving the ladder. Then, over-balancing, the ladder starts falling to the left. It was tilting about 45 degrees, *and falling fast.* My sister-in-law, Carol came around the corner and, seeing me and the ladder falling, planned on attempting to catch one or the other.

Immediately I found myself on the ground, holding the ladder, stopping its fall. Holding it long enough to yell *get out of the way.* When she was safely out of the way, the ladder came crashing down. If the Lord had not taken me down the ladder in supernatural time, and given me the strength to hold the ladder, it and I both would have landed on Carol, killing one or both of us. I knew then that there was no way I could climb down the ladder that fast unassisted. Years later, wondering if it would have been possible for me to have stopped the ladder unaided, I conducted an experiment.

I took a ladder of about the same size, extended it out the same length, balancing it straight up. Then, off-balancing it by a few degrees it would cause it to immediately crash down, I was completely unable to stop its fall no matter how hard I tried. While writing this account, I realized that Carol, like many others, may be unaware of how He saved her life.

Since I wrote the above, the Lord has revealed to me the sixth time He saved my life. It was also, not surprisingly, the first time. I was 16 or 17 at the time. I am now 69, so this happened some fifty years ago.

I was driving one night and crossed the train tracks behind the old Williams shoe factory in Portsmouth, Ohio. As I crossed the tracks, I found myself directly in the path of a very large train, so close that I could not see most of the front of the engine. It was way too close and going too fast for my 1956 *Chevy* to get clear. I floored the accelerator and cleared the track. On that night my car was super-charged. God had given it a power boost. This was unknown to me at the time. I felt no sensation other than that of acceleration.

My wife and I were passing thru Portsmouth late one night. We were one block from the crossing. A train blew its whistle, and I looked down the street toward the tracks, and saw this event occurring in less than vivid detail, more like a dream than a vision. In the time it took my car to pass through the intersection.

Thank you, Lord Jesus, for the last 50 years and all the blessings of my life.

TRIP TO ORLANDO

For several weeks, I thought it would be nice to visit some of my friends in Florida. Since we would not be in the South East again until November or December of 2017. Should we visit Paul, who lives in Daytona Beach, or Rita, Nelda, Maria and Nathan, who all live in the Orlando area? We were camping at *The Wells West*, light railroad and RV Resort in Silverhill, Alabama, an eight-hour drive from either city.

Since it was a long drive, Sharon did not want to go. We could not agree on whether we should go to Orlando, Daytona, or nowhere at all. I suggested that we should leave it up to God, by having our small church group from *Three Circle Church* in Daphne, Alabama, decide. If someone in the group should mention Orlando, there we would go, and if Daytona was mentioned, we would go there. If neither was mentioned, we would stay home. Within minutes of our small group starting one, of the men said, *"We are going to Disney in Orlando."* Daytona was not mentioned, which was strange. The *Daytona 500* race was on the television at the time.

Then we arrived in Orlando, I called Rita, who arranged for the six of us to meet at the *Denny's* where I had met them in 2014. While I was catching up with my friends, several things were happening, that I was not aware of.

At this point, Sharon will take over this narrative.

While my husband and I were meeting with several new acquaintances for a meal, I noticed that a few of the women were looking out the front window of the restaurant. When I looked out the window, I observed two women enthusiastically praying over one another.

When I was on my way back to my table from the restroom, one of the ladies (lady one) came into the restaurant. She was beaming. Her smile was the largest I had ever seen – even to this day. She was so excited, repeatedly saying things like "Glory to God," and "Praise God," and was moving quickly around the table where her friend was waiting for her. Her friend stood up, and they greeted each other with such enthusiasm that I cannot describe.

As I walked past them, lady one stopped me to tell me that I was a child of God, that God was happy with me, that I radiated His love, and that I was a special person.

Of course, I enjoyed her welcoming of me and observation of God's love in me. I filled up with God's love from her immediately. She told me that she would pray for me, and said she was praying for a husband for herself. I told her I would pray that God would for fulfil her prayer request. Then she turned back to her friend, and they sat down while I continued to my table.

I was distracted during my meal because it appeared as though each person that came into the restaurant was greeted with God's love by woman one. She was contagious, I tell you. There was more energy in the room because of her. I later asked her if she knew all these people, and she denied knowing any, other than the other lady sitting in the booth with her.

Sometime later, lady two came into the restaurant. I did not notice her until I was leaving. I had to pass by her, and when I recognized her as being the second woman on the street, I asked her if I could join her. Observing that she was journaling, I introduced myself, and asked about the praying encounter outside. She told me that she did not know lady one, but they had recognized each other as children of God.

She had met her on her way walking to another place in town. As she was coming back, she saw a burning flame on the concrete at the corner where the restaurant is located, a flame that she described as the fire of God, which drew her into the restaurant.

As we talked, she shared with me her history with the Lord and I shared mine. It was awesome. After this brief encounter, I left the restaurant filled with hope and joy, and had reaffirmed in the presence of the other believers just how good God is, and how much I am loved.

Both lady one and lady two had invited us to their churches. The following Sunday, my husband and I decided to go to lady one's church, as it was near the restaurant where we had eaten. We did not have specific directions to the church, but we knew we would find it. We decided to leave early enough to have breakfast on the way to church, in the same restaurant where I had encountered ladies one and two.

Dan and I sat at a booth. He ordered coffee as I was sitting down, then quickly said, *"We are in the wrong booth."* He pointed to lady two sitting in the same booth that she was sitting in the first time I met her. She was again journaling.

As I approached her, she sprang from her seat and began trying to tell me something exciting, but I was talking over her, also trying to tell her how excited I was to see her again. Still excited, we managed to sit down and calm ourselves. She smiled at me. Her eyes were sparkling. She passed her journal across the table and asked me to read the entry that she had made as we were walking into the restaurant. The entry said that she would receive a pleasant surprise today. I was her pleasant surprise, and she was mine. God is so good! By the way, she said she was led by The Spirit to eat at that restaurant, despite her church being on the other side of town.

Lady two knew where the church of lady one was located, and she gave us directions. We made it to the church and celebrated with the small congregation. After the service, lady one and my husband were talking on the other side of the room from me. During their conversation, lady one gave my husband a well-worn ring. When my husband gave me the ring, I immediately felt that it was very special to lady one, and that there was a deep connection between that ring and her life.

I approached lady one, and explained that I didn't want to offend her but that I couldn't keep her ring, as I felt it was of significance to her. Lady one began to cry and explained that this was the ring that she wore and spun it as she prayed for her husband. I was blessed to hear the Holy Spirit and refuse the ring.

What a wonderful time in my life to live in the truth of God's love story.

A PRIVATE JOKE

I was having a spiritual awakening, God had brought me closer to Him than I had ever believed possible. In fact, I had heard His voice on several occasions in the preceding months. It is beneficial to hear His voice, offering positive direction, and not just negative proscriptions; telling me what to do, and not only what not to do.

I had just finished shopping for some building materials from a Big-box store. I was pulling out onto the road, intending to turn right to head back to the job. I then heard His quiet voice say, *"Go and get yourself some new jeans."* Knowing exactly where to go, I turned to the left. Since I always shop at second hand stores, and there was a Goodwill store adjacent.

I went inside and proceeded to the men's area, finding three pairs of jeans in my size, all brand new, still with the original store price tags on them. He had put it on some one's heart to donate three new pairs of jeans.

There was something a little unusual about them. These jeans had pockets for an old-style carpenter's rule, a hammer loop, and an additional pocket for tools. So, the Lord enjoyed His little joke with me. Our Lord was a carpenter, and the adopted son of a carpenter. I am also the son of a carpenter, and something of a carpenter myself.

It is interesting and humorous that through Him, all things were made. He also enjoyed working with wood. His sharing of this joke with us, reveals how we are truly made in His image. Our Lord has, and has given us, a *sense of humor*. It also shows how much He cares for us, His children. I really needed some new jeans.

In addition, that pocket used for an old-style folding ruler has proven to be a great place to carry some *"TIME IS SHORT"* book marks to give to others.

We have an awesome God who gives to each of us all we need out of His love. May we return His love and caring, first to Him, and then to our neighbors. To God goes the glory and the last laugh, and my thanks for the new jeans.

IT IS GOING TO BE A RAINY DAY

Rita was at work one day, when a man from Australia came into her store. He was a bit apprehensive as he explained an experience he had just had with his Aboriginal traveling companion. They had been sitting on a park bench, and when a squirrel came close, his friend caught it and broke its neck, planning on taking it back to their hotel room for dinner.

He explained to his friend that they don't do things like that in the US, and that they could be arrested.

I am sure his friend thought Americans must be crazy to waste perfectly good food. This experience made our friend from Down Under realize how the culturally difference could cause real problems, but he had business to attend to that required his leaving his friend at the hotel alone.

While talking to Rita, he wondered out loud what kind of trouble, if any, his friend would cause. Rita told me that for some unknown reason she needed to speak in tongues. When she did, he asked her how she knew how to speak his dialect. She told him she didn't speak any Australian Aboriginal dialects. He said, "You just did, and you said it is going to be a rainy day." She then explained to him about the gift of tongues from the Holy Spirit, which he had never heard of, as he was, at that time, an unbeliever. The Holy Spirit gave her a symbolic answer to his question, that indeed there would be some problems come up, like clouds on a rainy day.

Our God is so amazing that He revealed His power to a man who didn't know Him, and a visitor to our country just making a small purchase at a store. I am sure that this man had many questions about what had just happened. I am positive that this occurred for this man to awaken from slumber. He will have to arrive at his own answer, just as we all must. The people who have shared their testimonies in this book have their answer. Do you?

Dan's notation:

In this chapter, many attributes of God are shown to us. How His Plan overlooks nothing. When He wishes someone to be somewhere, He makes a way. He is patient for 30 years to have a rosary delivered. In His love, He gives blessings; both small and large. A piece of pie, money, discounts fights, and everything we need. He also is the God who gives and takes away, and remember; He also has a sense of humor.

"Therefore I tell you, do not worry about your life, what you will eat or drink: or about your body, what you will wear. Is not life

more than food, and the body more important than clothes?"
Matthew 6:25

Section Two

Time is Short and What May Be

Chapter Seven

TIME IS SHORT; THE MESSAGE

In brief, *Time is Short* is a message from the Holy Spirit, given at a men's retreat on October17th, 2014. A message given for all Christians.

The church I attend when I live in southern Ohio is *Clear Mountain Community Church*, a small non-denominational congregation, located in Williamsburg. It is the tradition of *CMCC* to have both a men's and women's retreat each year.

At my wife's insistence, I attended the 2013 retreat. The retreat was going as I expected, until I met Scott, a friend and guest of Pastor Mark. His story was of his overcoming of an alcohol addiction, and leaving a high-paying career to serve the Lord. His very emotional response to our Lord's love touched me deeply. I had, unknown to others in my church, a struggle with sex addiction years previous, which had left me with many unresolved issues. Seeing what he had, I wanted it also.

Following the 2013 retreat, I personally had four prayer requests. The first was that I would bring one person to *CMCC* who had never been there before. The second was to bring one person to Christ in my lifetime. The third to receive the gift of tongues, specifically the ability to interpret tongues, so I could be of service to my church. The fourth was that I would do the good works that the Lord had planned for me to do before time began, plus a few more to make up for wasted years.

As the year progressed, I was looking forward to the 2014 retreat, until about three months before the retreat was to be held. Sharon and I had desired and planned for years to visit all fifty states together. With this goal in mind, we decided to do one more house renovation and refurbishment, and to sell our home. Then we would use this money to pay for our trip. With two houses to work on, I started worrying that I wouldn't have time for the retreat. One of the enemy's many tricks; when you want to do something good, he will often place many obstacles in your path. They are not evil or sinful, just everyday business. The enemy can use them to keep you from your greater good.

Sharon, seeing my change in attitude, started to pray that I would be able to attend, that I would ride down with someone else so that I would *have to* stay, which is what happened. I decided to go. I went to the church to get directions, so I could drive myself, and could leave early if I wanted. Then at the church, as Sharon had prayed and the Holy Spirit directed, I accepted a ride with a good friend. Thanks be to God for answered prayers.

The Holy Spirit moved powerfully at the 2014 retreat. On Friday during a 15-minute prayer time; I heard as many as six times, *He is coming*. I said nothing, and in a few minutes, he arrived. It had been my intention to ask a church elder to pray over me for my planned trip. I wanted to ask for God's protection, and the courage to speak His word to any unbelievers we might meet along the way.

As I was approaching the elder – I was just a little to his left and slightly behind him – when another church member, Jack, was approaching him from his front. Both men then fell at the same moment, pushed by some unseen force. The elder fell face-first toward the other man. Jack fell in the opposite direction, falling back to where the elder had been. They never touched until they were on the floor. Picture, if you will, running forward and falling backward. Both men fell in perfect coordination. Jack fell backward, and he hit his head on a metal folding chair, so hard that I thought he would be seriously injured. I had never seen anything like this before. I went out into the hallway for a much needed a drink of water. When I returned, others were on the floor. Later, I would learn that other men had received the Holy Spirit while I was in the hallway. A little while later, we retired to our cabins.

The next day, the Holy Spirit would give us His message. On Saturday, I remembered that I did not have the opportunity to ask the elder to pray over me. I went in search of him; I searched in the other cabins on the grounds, the chapel, and he was nowhere to be found. I returned to my cabin, and there he was, standing on the front porch. I asked him to pray for me, never dreaming how my life would be changed in the next few minutes. He agreed to pray with me and suggested we go inside, and we did.

The elder started to pray over me, when Jack, the other man who had fallen over the night before, came in and joined him. As they prayed over me in both English and in tongues, the elder said that he was feeling resistance, from something that had been there a long time. Then, he cast out a demon I had no idea was there. As they were praying, another man, Dean, came in and prayed for me to receive the armor of God: precisely what I had asked the elder to pray for me.

I believe that the demon cast out had been there to try to prevent what happened next, to attempt to keep my life from taking its new course. As they continued to pray over me, I started to hear – softly at first, then with ever increasing volume – I started speaking softly, then increasingly louder, and with outstretched arms, *"Time is Short."*

The voice that was speaking was mine, but also not mine. The Holy Spirit was giving us a message that, indeed, *time is short*. I later learned that as this was occurring, Scott had come in; the man who had such a profound effect on me the previous year.

After I finished speaking, I sat down on a couch, then once again, felt an indescribable feeling of peace and contentment, one that only comes from God. This was an overwhelming experience, and later that night I was unable to sleep. I knew I had to share with the others what the Lord had said.

RETREAT TESTIMONY

What follows is my first account, as given at the men's retreat.

Please bear with me, as speaking in public is something that is difficult for me. The other day, I sought out brother Tom for a simple prayer request to strengthen me for a good work that I believe has been set before me. It wasn't so simple after all. There was a demon in me, and Tom felt that it had been there for a long time. I think that is why I felt that my walk was more of a roller coaster ride than a walk. As others prayed with us and I received the Holy Spirit, He gave me this message that *time is short:* three words only. So, we must start moving. I don't have anything else to say except that I have no idea *how short time is*. I am sure we have time to act because this is a *call to action* for us all.

After I finished giving this brief testimony, one of the men, Steve, (who would later become a good friend) gave me a medal. On one side was a Christian, dressed in Roman body armor. On the other side was Ephesians, listing spiritual connotations on each of the armor parts. Steve some weeks later explained that for some unknown reason, he felt the need to bring this medal to the retreat. He had this medal for years, but he somehow knew to bring it along.

While we were cleaning up, Dean, the third man to pray on me, was passing out bookmarks that he had prepared for the retreat. On the bookmarks were, again, a man in body armor and the same scripture from Ephesians. So powerfully was the Holy Spirit working with this group of men, both before and during the retreat, that so many were drawn to this passage in Ephesians.

On my way home, I called my wife to inform her of all that transpired at the retreat. She asked if she could tell her sister Tina. Tina is a person of great faith, a person who has *Full Reliance On God*: a *FROG*. I initially responded in the negative, thinking Tina would think I am crazy, when the Holy Spirit reminded me that His message was not for me alone, and that I should share it with her and everyone. Perhaps that is part of His plan to use this book to share His message with you.

BOOKMARK EXPLAINED

After arriving home from the retreat, I spent a lot of time in prayer, asking for a way to give the testimony that was all of Him and none of me. Even more pressing was that His message that *Time is Short* is a call to action. What action Lord? I prayed as to what specific action He wanted us to take.

All praise and thanks to the Lord. He answers prayers! In only a few short weeks and the most blessed of my life. He was guiding and talking to me constantly. He answered this prayer and the four previously mentioned prayers, all between late October of 2014 to January 5th of 2015. If He would have used someone other than me, I imagine it would have only taken a couple of days. He has always been very patient with me.

He answered the question, what action Lord, what specific action do you want us to do? On the bookmark entitled "TIME IS SHORT".

TIME IS SHORT

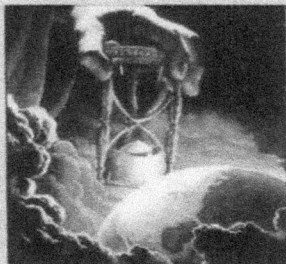

Genesis 1:14 Signs in heaven.

Acts 2:17-20 And it shall come to pass in the last days, says GOD, That I will pour out My Spirit on all flesh; your sons and your daughters shall prophesy, your young men shall see visions, your old men shall dream dreams. And on My menservants and maidservants I will pour out My Spirit in those days; and they shall prophesy. I will show wonders in heaven above and signs in the earth beneath: blood and fire and vapor of smoke. The sun shall be turned into darkness, and the moon into blood, before the great and awesome day of the Lord.

TIME IS SHORT

Message from the Spirit of God

Romans 13:11-13 Awaken from sleep and put on the armor of light.

1 Cor. 7:29-31 *Time is short* and the form of this world is passing away.

Isa. 9 The bricks have fallen.

Dan. 9 Repent and understand His truth.

1 Cor. 14 Pursue spiritual gifts.

Rev. 1:1-3 The Revelation of Jesus Christ of things which must *shortly* take place...for the *time is near.*

Rev. 22:7, 10, 20 Behold, I am *coming quickly!* Do not seal the words of the prophecy of this book, for the *time is at hand.* He who testifies to these things says, "Surely I am *coming quickly.*" Amen. Even so, come, Lord Jesus!

Dan's notation:

I often tell people that God wrote the bookmark entitled *TIME IS SHORT*, as the entire bookmark is made up of Bible passages, and of summaries of bible passages, that God wrote it is self-evident. It would be more correct to say that He chose the passages, their order, and their meaning.

In brief, *Time is Short* is a message from the Holy Spirit, given during a Christian men's retreat in October of 2014: a message given for all.

The first verse found on the bookmark is also one of the first verses of the Bible:

*And God said, "Let there be lights in the expanse of the sky to separate the day from the night, and let them serve as signs to mark seasons and days and years." **Genesis 1:14***

This first verse is where God tells us that He has placed signs in the sky to notify us of important events. The star of Bethlehem announced our Savior's birth, for the best known example. These verses also foretell of man's fall, for if man wasn't going to fall, there would be no need for signs. The Lord would have walked with us and told us what He wanted to impart directly, through the Holy Spirit.

Acts 2:17-20 again carries on the themes of signs in the heavens.

In the last days, God says, I will pour out My Spirit on all people. Your sons and your daughters will prophesy, your young men will see visions, your old men will dream dreams. Even on my servants, both men and women, I will pour out My Spirit in those days, and they prophesy. I will show wonders in heaven above and signs in the earth below, blood and fire and billows of smoke. The sun will be turned to darkness and the moon to blood before the coming of the great and glorious day of the Lord.

In these few verses, God establishes the past and the present, as Joel's prophecy foretold, and Peter's speech at Pentecost confirms: that the lasts days began with Christ's Death and Resurrection. So, just as it was true in Peter's day, how much less time is there now until our Lord's return?

TIME IS SHORT. This is the message from the Spirit of God, given to us at the men's retreat.

Within the next verses, He tells us the first action required of us: to awaken from sleep and put on the armor of light.

And do this, understanding the present time. The hour has come for you to wake up from your slumber, because our salvation is nearer now than we first believed. The night is nearly over; the day is almost here. So, let us put aside the deeds of darkness and put on the armor of light. Let us behave decently as in the daytime, not in orgies and drunkenness, not in sexual immorality and debauchery, not in dissension and jealousy. **Romans13:11-13**

Even before He gave us His message, He was urging us all to don the armor of God: note the number of people drawn to **Ephesians 6:10-20** before and during the retreat.

Finally, be strong in the Lord and His mighty power. Put on the full armor of God, so you can take your stand against the devil's schemes. Ephesians 6:10

As **1 Corinthians 7:29-31** tells us, *Time is Short*, and the form of this world is passing away.

This verse tells us how we are to approach this time:

What I mean, brothers, is that time is short. From now on those who have wives should live as if they had none; those who mourn, as if they did not; those who are happy, as if they were not; those who buy something, as if it were not theirs to keep; those who use the things of the world, as if not engrossed in them. For this world in its present form is passing away.

Isaiah 9:10 tells us how the bricks have fallen.

"The bricks have fallen down, but we will rebuild with dressed stone; the fig-trees have been felled, but we will replace them with cedars."

Previous to this, **Isaiah 9:**2 tells us how the people walking in darkness have seen a great light.

The people walking in darkness have seen a great light; on those living in the land of the shadow of death a light has dawned.

Isaiah 9:6 continues on to state that to us a child is born, unto us a son is given; and the government shall be upon his shoulders.

For to us a child is born, to us a son is given, and the government will be on his shoulders. And he will be called Wonderful Counsellor, Mighty God, Everlasting Father, Prince of Peace.

These scriptures demonstrate that this prophecy is for us, as well as the people of long ago. At the time of its writing, Jesus had not yet come. Daniel 9 admonishes us to repent and understand His truth.

So, I turned to the Lord God, and pleaded with Him in prayer and petition, in fasting, and in sackcloth and ashes. I prayed to the LORD my God and confessed: "Oh Lord, the great and awesome God who keeps his covenant of love with all who love him and obey his commands, we have sinned and done wrong. We have been wicked and have rebelled; we have turned away from your commands and laws. **Daniel 9:3-5**

Isaiah 9 is our warning, and Daniel 9 is a call to change our ways. **1 Corinthians 12** admonishes us to pursue spiritual gifts and verse 1 emphasizes the importance of these spiritual gifts:

Now about spiritual gifts, brothers, I do not want you to be ignorant. Therefore, I tell you to know that no-one who is speaking by the Spirit of God says, "Jesus be cursed," and no one can say, and no-one can say "Jesus is Lord," except by the Holy Spirit. **1 Corinthians 12:3**

To one there is given through the Spirit the message of wisdom, to another the message of knowledge by means of the same Spirit, to another faith by the same Spirit, to another gifts of healing by that one Spirit, to another miraculous powers, to another prophecy, to another distinguishing between spirits, to another speaking in different kinds of tongues, and to still another the interpretation of tongues. All these are the work of one and the same Spirit, and he gives them to each one, just as He determines. ***1 Corinthians 12:8-11***

1 Corinthians 14:1 continues to tell us about the gifts of prophecy and speaking in tongues.

Follow the way of love and eagerly desire spiritual gifts, especially the gift of prophecy.

1 Corinthians 14:22 continues:

Tongues, then, are a sign, not for believers but for unbelievers; prophecy, however, is for believers, not for unbelievers.

First, we must awaken, and prepare ourselves for spiritual battle; don our spiritual armor of God, and make haste to do what is right in the eyes of God. To pursue the spiritual gifts, especially the higher gifts of prophecy, discerning of tongues, healing and the working of miracles, and of course *faith* and *love*.

The revelation of Jesus Christ, which God gave him to show his servants what must soon take place. He made it known by sending his angel to his servant John, who testifies to everything he saw – that is, the word of God and the testimony of Jesus Christ. Blessed is the one who reads the words of this prophecy, and blessed are those who hear it and take to heart what is written in it, because the time is near. ***Revelation 1:1-3***

*"Behold, I am coming soon!" Blessed is he who keeps the words of the prophecy in this book." **Revelation 22:7***

*Then he told me, "Do not seal up the words of the prophecy of this book, because the time is near." **Revelation 22:10***

He who testifies to these things says, "Yes, I am coming soon."
Amen. come, Lord Jesus. **Revelation 22:20**

HOW THE PASSAGES WERE CHOSEN

The title of the bookmark, the message from the Holy Spirit, witnessed in its entirety by myself and two others, and partially by two more.

I am no bible scholar; not now, and certainly less so when the bookmark was written. The scriptures taken from Genesis and Acts show that from the beginning, our God placed signs in the heavens that would be made clear in the last days. They fit so perfectly that they required inclusion, directly inspired by the Holy Spirit. Note the signs in heaven mentioned in Genesis, in Acts, and in Revelation.

The selection from Romans was added due to the number of times the Armor of God came up during the retreat.

The sections from Isaiah were added when three or four people encouraged me to read *The Harbinger* by Jonathan Kahn one Sunday, both before and after services. Though these people all knew me, they were in different social groups, and may or may not have known each other. This was between October of 2014 and January 5th of 2015. *The Harbinger* was written some three years prior. To my knowledge, it had not been in the public eye for years. In the book, Mr. Kahn points out the supernatural similarity of Isaiah's prophecy on Israel and the 9-11 attack on the World Trade Center.

The section from chapter 9 of the book of Daniel was added after I was sleeping, and woke hearing a voice that said, *"Wake up and read Daniel 9 and pray it over your country."* I had no idea what was written in Daniel chapter 9 until I read it that night.

Corinthians 14, with its call to pursue spiritual gifts was the last passage to be added. It came to be included in the following manner. About two weeks after the retreat, I was driving on State Route 28, in Goshen, Ohio. I had just passed a restaurant, *The J & J*, or *The Double J*, when I heard a voice say, *"Turn around and have lunch there."* I did, and the food there was very good. When I was almost finished eating, a man came in and sat down behind me. I was preparing to leave when I looked at him, and I had a strange feeling that I knew him. After we talked for a few minutes, we agreed that we couldn't have known each other.

Once outside, I felt I was missing something. I went back in. When I looked at him, he said, *"Yes, you know me, I am a fellow Christian."* I asked if we could talk for a moment, and he said he *"always wants to talk to one of the elect."*

He then told me that he had received a call to come to this restaurant about 20 minutes earlier.

I told him of my recent retreat experience: that three men prayed over me in English and in tongues. When I said tongues, he said, *"Hold on there"* somewhat taken aback. He belonged to one of the churches that believe that the gifts died out with the Apostles, or that tongues come from the devil, or are just gibberish, I do not know which. We agreed to disagree on this point.

We talked for a while as he finished eating. Outside, he gave me one of the first testimonies I received for this book (Addict Sent Back) and I would learn later, much more. I had no idea at that time I would be doing this book. He told me about his son. His son had a drug addiction and had overdosed near a first responder building. When they arrived to help him, he had already turned blue, and stayed that way as they worked on him for six more minutes. When he regained consciousness, he said, *"I did not see God, but I heard Him say 'I do not want you to die in this manner, so go back.'"* Back he came free of his addiction.

I had never met anyone who had a family member come back from the dead. I was so overwhelmed that I went and recounted the tale for my pastor. I would soon learn that the Lord was going to have many more people share their testimonies with us.

Weeks later, while putting the bookmark together, knowing that it was almost finished, but still missing part of His call to action. That most central call to action, because *Time is Short*. I was overcome by a brilliant insight, which must have come from the Holy Spirit. If there is one thing that all men can agree on, it is that I am not particularly brilliant.

The testimony that I thought to be the reason for our encounter, important as it was, was not the key thing I was meant to learn. What my brother was missing, the gifts of the Spirit, 1 Corinthians 14 was the missing action and missing passage. With its addition, the bookmark was completed.

Much later, while writing this account, I remembered that we had not spoken of the Lord until I came back into the restaurant, yet he knew that I was a Christian. Was this a display of this man's gift of spiritual discernment; one of the gifts of the Holy Spirit?

To the unbeliever, or some Christian skeptics, it would be easy to assume that I started writing the bookmarks, taking only chosen passages to support a preconceived notion. Nothing could be further from the truth. I was not a student of the bible, and mine had not been opened in months; just sitting there, gathering dust.

Furthermore, I lack the computer skills necessary to make the files in printable form, I type using only the *hunt and peck* method. If it wasn't for spell check, you likely wouldn't be able to read this. With the necessary skills lacking in me, God gave me someone to meet the need, even before I knew such a need existed. The Lord walks ahead of us.

Dean, the third person to pray on me at the retreat, had to move out of his apartment at short notice. I had a second house I was restoring, so I asked Dean to house sit for me, while I finished the project. Dean moved into the project house and provided the missing digital expertise. I would sometimes ask him what it felt like to be kidnapped by the Holy Spirit to work on the bookmarks? He would reply that *it was great*.

Dean, far more than myself, was responsible for completing the bookmarks. He searched the internet to find just the right images to convey the message, summarizing bible verses into a few words. He was always patient with me as I made alterations to it, as the Lord revealed the passages He wanted.

Chapter Eight

Dreams

What follows has been included only after much prayer seeking guidance as to what the Lord wanted me to do with the five dream testimonies I had received. The other testimonies in this book are of the present or past, whereas the dream testimonies may be of the future. The Lord is ever faithful in answering my prayers.

While shopping in a general store in a small Wyoming town, the Lord blessed me by introducing to me two young ladies, one of whom had the answer to my prayer.

The young lady was working the cash register, and we began to talk, first about her plans to buy some cattle and start her own ranch. She then told me about a mark of the beast dream she'd had.

CHIP TESTIMONY FROM WYOMING

I'm not quite sure what I was praying about before I had this dream. Sometimes I pray so long that I accidentally fall asleep before I say Amen. Whoops! This dream was different from any other dream I've ever had. There wasn't much substance to the dream, most of my surroundings appeared to be gray or white, like I was in a sepia tone picture. I believe the location was a grocery store.

The counter top was gray, and so were the walls and floor. I was standing in line waiting to pay for my groceries. When it was my turn, I passed my right wrist over a scanner and my groceries were paid for. Someone was asking me about my 'chip.' I can remember telling them that even if I wanted to take the chip out, I couldn't, because it was embedded in my artery. The weird thing was, there were beings in this dream, but I can't recall faces our names, but they were there, somewhere lost in the background.

Dan's notation:

When I first met this young lady, she didn't tell me the details of this dream. She asked me if I thought that the enemy could force someone to take the mark. Given the nature of this dream, and the fact that she is a Christian, her question is very understandable. I responded that since having the mark means damnation, I didn't believe that God would let anyone physically force the mark on you.

After further deliberation, I reconsidered my answer, and I felt I needed to give her a warning. While physical force is ruled out, the enemy could perhaps coerce you, by threatening harm to your loved ones for example. We need to remember that the mark is not to be accepted under any circumstance, and we need to pray for grace. I warned her to pray, pray for the grace of a martyr for herself and her family.

In the Catholic Bible, Second Maccabees Chapter 7, is the martyrdom of a mother and her sons, an example of faith over torture.

I went back to my camper to get them a few testimonies to read. I gave them my email address and asked if she would send me her dream testimony because dreams count too. It was the next day I that realized this was the answer to my prayer. The dreams are included. You can decide for yourself if they have meaning or not.

WILD DOGS

When in Israel, two young women shared with us their dreams, one German lady, and the other an American. The German lady experienced her dream in her own country. The American experienced hers in Israel, and the dream was set in the old city.

These two dreams were strikingly similar, excepting their locations. In both dreams, the women were being chased by packs of dogs, both women were leading children and babies, and were trying to reach a safe place, going up stairs to either a church or a temple.

"For this is what the Sovereign Lord says: How much worse will it be when I send against Jerusalem, my four dreadful judgements – sword and famine and wild beasts and plague – to kill its men and their animals!" **Ezekiel 14:21**

Dan's notation:

The dreams are of dogs, you say. Remember the commercial: in the heart of every dog is a wolf. There are more wild animals in the developed world than you may think. In the United States, there are over 20000 mountain lions, 10000 African lions and tigers, 200,000 black bears, and 5700 gray wolves, not counting what is in Alaska. Not to mention coyotes, which are everywhere. Plus, hundreds of millions of dogs. More than enough for Him to pour out His judgement on us using animals if He desires.

Reading my notes on the dreams, I wonder why I couldn't see then what is now obvious. **Acts 2:17-18**:

"Your old men will dream dreams. Even on my servants, both men and women, I will pour out my Spirit in those days."

His pouring out of His Spirit may be why two of the young women's dreams were so similar. All of the dreams share an end times connection.

MARK OF THE BEAST

Another dream relayed to us came from a young woman, Maria, in Ohio, within a few weeks of the retreat. I was watching this lady at work, thinking to myself that watching her is like watching Him. She would move from one group of coworkers, to customers, to another group, and wherever she went, people's spirits were lifted. I have met many good Christians in the last few years, but none moved me in the way that this young woman did. It would be easy to think that she was an angel, as others have mentioned in this book, but she is human just like us. Yet she and I both believe that the Lord has something very special in mind for her. We both, at the same moment, exclaimed that He did.

In her dream, Maria was standing in a long line. A young man was having people pass their hands through a scanning device. When it became her turn, she and the young man started talking. He asked her a question, what the question was is unknown to me. She told me that due to its phrasing she could answer truthfully.

He then became distracted, and passed her through without scanning her hand. She then proceeds down a long corridor, that opened into a

Roman-style Colosseum, with a stage in the middle. On the stage, there was someone that first appeared as a man, but she could see that he was, in fact, an alien dragon. There were six of her friends on stage also, who were beheaded by the alien dragon as she watched.

NEW TEMPLE

One of my two dreams that occurred after the retreat in October 2014. In this dream, I am a very old man. My hair and beard are completely gray almost white. I am standing talking to two others, who, I believe, are the two witnesses. We are all dressed in robes, mine darker than the others. The dream was in black and white, so the robe colors are unknown. My view of this scene is from above and behind myself, in the third person. We are standing and talking by a pool of water, that I knew was on the front left side of the third temple, even though I had never seen the temple.

On my trip to the Holy Land, Sharon and I stayed at a Hampton Inn in Atlantic City, where we met Lisa. Lisa told me that I will live to be very old and that I will have a gray beard and hair. At the time of this meeting, I did not have a beard. I started growing one just to see how gray it would be. Note that Lisa's statement, seemingly an unrelated event, supports the dream.

While in Jerusalem, I visited *The Temple Institute*. They have a scale model of their planned new temple, that they will build after God does some demo work on the Temple Mount. This model has a pool of water on both front sides of the Temple.

There was one thing different in my dream: the pool had a different shape. In one, it is round, whereas in the other it is square. I cannot recall if it was round or square in the dream.

WHAT WAS OURS

My other dream occurred while I was taking a rare nap. In this dream, a man dressed as an American pioneer was making a speech to a group of people. He said, *"What was ours is ours again, and will never be taken from us again."* Immediately after this dream, I went to look up the size of Israel in the time of King David. I thought this was a strange dream to have. I knew where I had heard these words before. Before I reveal where and how, I believe some background is in order.

Following the retreat, some strange things happened. In their order of occurrence, the first was that I would become very emotional and cry whenever I felt the Lord's involvement in things. While scanning radio stations, a song played for just a few seconds, and I started to cry. I had heard this song many times in the past, and it never previously affected me. The song is entitled *"I have never known love like this before"* by Stephanie Mills, who sang at *Brooklyn Cornerstone Baptist Church* as a child. I stopped the scan and listened to the whole song.

This song could easily be about the Holy Spirit. Over the next couple of hours, I listened to other so-called love songs that could also be about Him.

Having seen His hand in music, I wondered if He did the same in movies. I downloaded a list of the 250 most popular movies and discovered that there are patterns there.

The first five movies on the list are *The Shawshank Redemption*, key word redemption. The second is *The Godfather*, and the third movie *The Godfather Part Two*. The fourth movie is *The Dark Knight*. The fifth is *Pulp Fiction*. This is the pattern that I saw: first the Redemption, the single most important event in history. Second, the Redemption as foretold by God the Father in the old testament. Thirdly, Redemption given to us by God in the new testament. Numbers four and five, *The Dark Knight* and *Pulp Fiction*. Satan is the dark knight, and his lies are the pulp fiction. Note that they come below Redemption and God.

Redemption and Spring, Summer, Fall, Winter, and then Spring. Read it this way: Redemption, God in the beginning as the spring, creation of man as the summer, the fall as the fall of man, the winter now, and the spring the Second coming.

There are other patterns, some easy to notice, others not so much.

A few weeks after downloading the list of movies, my wife, myself, and two friends visited Saint Augustine, Florida, where we went in a souvenir shop. I found myself looking at a map of ship wrecks off the Florida coast. I really had to have this map, strange as I am not typically a purchaser of souvenirs, especially over-priced ones. I bought it anyway regardless of price, I had to have it.

The next day, I stared at the map, wondering why I had to have it. It was then that I noticed several ship wrecks with movie or TV themed names: *Casablanca*, *John Wayne*, *Enterprise*, and *Gunsmoke*. Some of the wrecks on the map had dates written next to them.

One of the ships was *The Enterprise*, June 5, 1859. The Enterprise is related to my dream. The man dressed as a pioneer in my dream was a scene from the original series of Star Trek that I had seen some decades before.

Just to the right of the Enterprise, there is an illustration of another ship called *The Maple Leaf* with another movie connection. *The Maple Leaf* was a steamship, with two smoke stacks billowing black smoke in the illustration. When it sank, it was being used as a prison ship, which put me in mind of the movie *Lock, Stock, and Two Smoking Barrels*.

Getting back to the dream, the man in the dream said, *"What was ours before is ours again and will never be taken from us again."* This, I believe, is about Israel, and that God will return it to the people He gave it to, in its entirety.

You now have the dream and my interpretation of it, but it doesn't end there, and includes more related events. *The Enterprise*, and the date on the map, June 5th. On June 5th, 2015, while in Louisville, Kentucky, I saw the *Belle of Louisville* blow black smoke from its twin towers. It blew smoke for only a few seconds while it was tied to the dock. On June the 5th, 2016, nothing happened, to my surprise. On the 6th of June of 2016, while in Mystic Seaport in Connecticut, Sharon and I went to see what we thought was a replica of *The Mayflower*, that turned out to be the replica of the slave ship *La Amistad*, which brought to mind again the movie *Lock, Stock, and Two Smoking Barrels*.

Nothing happened on either the 5th or 6th of June in 2017, though on June 7th, while reading the news, an article came on discussing the best Star Trek movies. As previously stated, I believe that the dream refers to Israel, and to its permanence and growth and return to the size of King David's empire, and soon. I further believe that the events of the past three Junes, particularly from the 5th to the 7th, is the Lord's way of telling me that my interpretation is correct. My belief in this is further strengthened by the title of the Star Trek episode. "The Omega Glory", or glory at the end. By the way, June 5th, 1967, was the start of the Six Days War, in which Israel was expanded. On June the 8th of 2018, nothing happened, perhaps because He had given me three signs already.

It was on a trip, the week of March 8th, 2015, that I met Nathan, a prophet. In the weeks prior, I kept seeing things about *The USS Oriskany*, a scuttled Essex-class aircraft carrier, carefully sunk off the Florida coast, plus I was meeting a surprising number of ladies named Regina, my mother's middle name. I saw several articles about the ship, saw men wearing Oriskany hats, and met two men not wearing their hats, who had served aboard her. Since she had been scuttled off the coast of Florida, I looked on the map, and there she was. Having located the Oriskany on the map, I looked to see what it could mean, but there were no dates listed for her. Now what do I do? A few days later, I again looked at the map, and noticed that she was in 210 feet of water. While following down the coast, looking at the water level of 200 feet, I noticed *The Regina*. *The Regina* is not in 200 feet, but 50, and she just jumped out for me. The Regina has the date of March 8th, and the location of Longboat Key. That is why we made this trip to Florida and Longboat Key during that week.

There are hundreds of other ships on this map. In the years following this trip, none of them have been brought to my attention. Many coincidences, you may say, could explain this. Just one more thing: I do not believe in coincidences, as God oversees all.

Back to the Florida trip, my friend John and I were using metal detectors on this trip. On Flagger beach I found a wire star with a tail, a dolphin pendant, and I picked up a plastic whale. We also saw a space launch, something I had always wanted to see. God gives us our hearts' desires, and this was one of mine.

Several weeks later, a man I met at church named Jeff and I, took the one-week trip to Florida. This was the trip that we met Nathan. We left his house heading west on route 125, a shooting star passed directly over us, heading west. Jeff commented that it much be a sign from above that the Lord was blessing our trip. On the beach, I saw a single dolphin swim by. Jeff told me that his wife's maiden name was Whale. All three of my finds on the beach accounted for.

This was where I planned on ending this book until a few days ago. September 14, 2017, I was going to stop my writing and just wait for the Lord to give us a few more testimonies to include. I felt that I had passed on all I could. That was until someone asked me what I thought would happen on September 23, 2017, and I asked her what she was talking about. She said the sign in the heavens in Revelation 12, verses one and two, will occur on the 23rd of September. I had completely forgotten about it. My friend Steve had told me about it over a year previous, as he is very interested in such things. She said she wondered if the Lord would be returning on the 23rd. I told her that I believed nothing supernatural would occur on this day, if it is the sign in Revelation 12, then it is only a sign, and that Christ's return is near, but that we still have time to continue His mission.

Chapter Nine

Prophecies of His Return

PROPHECIES OF HIS RETURN

Knowing that *time is short*, I wondered if there were any prophecies given to others that would support or disprove my belief that we are living in last the decades before Jesus returns. I searched for End Times prophecies. First looking for the prophecies contained in the bible, I found many, some of which will be included abridged with just some of the predictions that we can see have been, or are being, fulfilled.

> *"You looked, O king, and there before you stood a large statue —
> an enormous, dazzling statue, awesome in appearance. The head
> of the statue was made of pure gold, its chest and arms of silver, its
> belly and thighs of bronze, its legs of iron, its feet partly of iron and
> partly of baked clay. While you were watching, a rock was cut out,
> but not by human hands. It struck the statue on its feet of iron and
> clay and smashed them. Then the iron and the clay, the bronze, the
> silver and the gold were all broken to pieces at the same time and
> became like chaff on a threshing-floor in the summer. The wind
> swept them away without leaving a trace. But the rock that struck
> the statue became a huge mountain and filled the whole earth."*
> ***Daniel 2:31-35***

> *But you, Daniel, close up and seal the words of the scroll until the
> time of the end. Many will go here and there to increase knowledge.*
> ***Daniel 12:4***

People now travel all over the world, and it is easy to see that man's knowledge has expanded in every area. Ever learning, and yet never able to come to the knowledge of the truth: human knowledge increases with the exception of the knowledge of His truth.

The Spirit clearly says that in latter times some will abandon the faith and follow deceiving spirits and things taught by demons. 1 **Timothy 4:1**

How have we departed from the faith; many now believe in evolution, a teaching unknown in Timothy's time. The increase of secular living, the increasing number of atheists. Political correctness that demands every faith be considered the same. This one is particularly dangerous. It discourages the spreading of the true gospel.

But mark this: There will be terrible times in the last days. People will be lovers of themselves, lovers of money, boastful, proud, abusive, disobedient to their parents, ungrateful, unholy, without love, unforgiving, slanderous, without self-control, brutal, not lovers of the good, treacherous, rash, conceited, lovers of pleasure rather lovers of God, having a form of godliness but denying its power. Have nothing to do with them. **2 Timothy 3:1-5**

These are terrible times, with worldwide terror attacks, riots, wars, school, church, and even waffle house shootings, as we are in constant peril, and no place is safe. Men have become lovers of their own selves, covetous, boasters, proud, blasphemers, disobedient to parents, unthankful, unholy, heady, high-minded, lovers of pleasures more than lovers of God. We are constantly buying things, trying to have it all. Do anything that will give us pleasure, we will drive for hours to go to a ball game, but a church ten minutes away is too far to attend.

First of all, you must understand that in the last days scoffers will come, scoffing and following their own evil desires. **2 Peter 3:3**

We meet these people everywhere; people who deny God, who believe in neither heaven nor hell, those who feel that only man is the judge of what is right or wrong, and that there is no higher power.

Don't let anyone deceive you by any way: for that day will not come until the rebellion occurs, and the man of lawlessness is revealed, the man doomed to destruction. He will oppose and will exalt himself over everything that is called God or is worshiped, so that he sets himself up in God's temple, proclaiming himself to be God. **2 Thessalonians 2:3-4**

It is likely that we all know someone who has fallen away from the church, and some churches which teach false doctrines. The anti-Christ, the son of perdition, some say has been revealed, though I personally believe this has not yet happened. If the temple of God referred to is the third temple in Jerusalem, it needs to be built.

At that time many will turn away from the faith and will betray and hate each other, and many false prophets will appear and deceive many people. Because of the increase of wickedness, the love of most will grow cold, but he who stands firm to the end will be saved. And this gospel of the kingdom will be preached in the whole world as a testimony to all nations, and then the end will come. **Matthew 24:10-14**

Many have turned away from the faith. Certainly, we all know someone who once believed, but now does not. This will increasingly occur, as Christians will have greater and greater pressure to conform to the world. Thanks to the hard work of missionaries and to the internet, the gospel is beginning to be known worldwide.

Now, this is what was spoken by the Apostle Peter;

"'In the last days, God says, I will pour out my Spirit on all people. Your sons and daughters will prophesy, your young men will see visions, your old men will dream dreams. Even on my servants, both men and women, I will pour out my Spirit in those days, and they will prophesy. I will show wonders in the heaven above and signs on the earth below, blood and fire and billows of smoke. The sun will be turned to darkness and the moon to blood before the coming of the great and glorious day of the Lord. And everyone who calls on the name of the Lord will be saved.'" **Acts 2:16-21** *Then He said to them: "Nation will rise against nation, and kingdom against kingdom. There will be great earthquakes,*

famines and pestilences in various places, and fearful events and great signs from heaven." **Luke 21:10**

A quick look at the news will show you that these things are occurring now, we just need to see if they start becoming more frequent and severe, as birth pangs increase in frequency as the baby's birth nears.

He also forced everyone, small and great, rich and poor, free and slave, to receive a mark on his right hand or on his foreheads, so that no-one could buy or sell unless he had the mark, which is the name of the beast or the number of his name. **Revelation 13:16-17**

Dan's notation:

A word of warning: if you search for End Times prophecies on the internet, you will find an incredible amount of misinformation. Every second we draw closer to His return, but that doesn't mean that every event has an End Times significance. If you spend any time searching the internet, you can find a great many suggestions as to how the prophecies should be interpreted, most of which contradict one another.

There has grown up an industry of End Times books, movies, and websites which esteem profits rather than truth, so be on guard when you read these things, and make sure that you compare them to His word in the Bible. That is also true for this book.

According to the website *Wikipedia*, there have been at least 175 dates predicting the End Times in the past. Some of these false predictions came from famous people. Pope Sylvester the Second, in the year 1000, Pope Innocent the Third in 1950, John Wesley in 1836, Jerry Falwell on January 1st of 2000, Martin Luther in 1600, Pat Robertson 1982...

I found site after site promoting one product or another, that were saying this Bible prophecy has been fulfilled or is being fulfilled.

WHAT IT ALL MEANS TO ME

Since receiving the message in 2014 that *Time is Short*, all the events which followed seemed to lead me to this point, and to writing this book. Before the men's retreat, people did not share their testimonies with me. Everything from the process of preparing the bookmarks, to the ordained meeting with the man in the restaurant, to meeting the prophet, the Jerusalem trip, complete with Blood Moon, meeting people with testimonies everywhere – has led me to this point.

This is what I believe; not something testified by His prophet, just one man's opinion. The front of the bookmark is the time in which we live; Romans, Daniel, and the verses from First Corinthians tell us what to do. Isaiah and Revelation tell us of what is soon to come. Genesis and Revelation show us how the beginning points toward the end, and how the end points to the beginning. The same with Acts 2:17-20 and 1 Corinthians chapter 14, The Lord says *I will pour out my Spirit in those days* (these days that we are currently living in). He tells us in First Corinthians chapter 14 to *seek His Spirit*. In a perfect self-sustaining loop – a perfect circle – as we pursue the Spirit, so will He will pour out His Spirit in a self sustaining way, constantly growing more powerful. As we draw closer and closer to the time of tribulation, our need for His Spirit will become greater, so that we may endure to the end.

I believe that the Lord has told us; through Isaiah chapter 9, and through the fall of the World Trade Center, that He has removed His hand – not only from the United States, but also the entire world. Note that it was the World Trade Center, and New York is home also to the United Nations Headquarters. The Trade Center buildings truly represented our current world order. He has done this for the same reasons He removed His protection from Jerusalem; our sins have reached clear to heaven: abortions, murders, rapes, robberies, sexual immorality, and on and on. Additionally, we no longer give Him what is due to Him alone. In a foolish quest for political correctness, we have said one god is equal to another, and that an idol is the equal of God. May Jesus have mercy on us, and may we turn back to Him.

This brings us to the Blood Moon; the last of the four that I witnessed while in Jerusalem. As Pastor Mark Blitz wrote, they are a sign from God, and something is going on. The question is how to interpret these signs. I look at this announcement as similar to any announcement that could be given about any event. The announcement could be of a future event (we are going to marry), a present event (are getting married), or an event already passed (we are married).

According to the book *Blood Moons: Decoding the imminent heavenly signs by* Pastor Mark Blitz (2014), the blood moons of 1492 and 1493 told of the Jews' expulsion from Spain, and the discovery of America, and a safe place for them to live. The 1949 and 1950 Blood Moons heralded Israeli statehood, and with the 1967 and '68 Blood Moons, Israel gained some control of Jerusalem, though lacking the control of the Temple Mount. I believe that the last of the tetrad of Blood Moons that occurred on September 28th of 2015 follows this pattern, and that Israel's control will be expanded; perhaps over the Temple Mount, or perhaps God will restore to the Jewish people all of the land that He promised to Abraham.

As I have said before, this is only my opinion, my interpretation of what He may be telling us. When you look at the Middle East today, you will see the enemies of Israel busy destroying each other, reminding me of Gideon and the three hundred; exhausted, yet keeping up the pursuit.

Either way, right or wrong, we will not have long to wait to find out. For *Time is Short*. I know because He told me.

ANOTHER ANGEL ENCOUNTER
Moments of Love

Vincent Tan was born Tan Ban Soon, in Singapore, to Chinese Buddhist parents. As a young boy, Vincent was very interested in science. One day, as he was reading a book on nuclear physics in the library, he discovered an offer for a Bible course stuck within the pages of the book. Curious, Vincent ordered the course. Ultimately, he became a Christian, and because he wanted to attend a Christian college, he came to the United States, and adopted for himself the Western name of Vincent.

Vincent graduated from college and took a job in analytic chemistry in Chattanooga, Tennessee. His faith deepened, possibly because he wasn't afraid to share it with others, and life settled down. In March of 1993, Vincent was working late in his lab, looking out the window occasionally to keep an eye on his car, because recently several had been stolen from the area. He noticed a stranger standing on the passenger side of his car. The man was young and clean cut, but thieves come in all guises, and because Vincent is proficient in martial arts, he decided to in investigate.

Grabbing a long metal rod from the lab, he opened the door and called, *"Yes? Can I help you?"*

"Hi, Vincent," the stranger responded.

Vincent was startled. Had he mistaken a friend for a thief? No, he had never seen this man before. *"Do I know you?"* Vincent asked.

"Not really." The man responded. *"But you don't have to use Chi Sao or the rod on me. And your mother is fine."*

Now Vincent was really confused. No one in America knew of his skill in Chi Sao, nor could the stranger see the rod Vincent held behind him. And who else could have known that his mother in China had just developed a heart problem?

The stranger smiled, *"You love the Lord very much, don't you?"*

"Yes, I do," Vincent answered. He started to relax.

"He loves you too," the man replied, *"And he is coming very soon."*

Vincent was thrilled. Could this be true? He looked away just for a second or two, and when he looked back, the man had disappeared.

Could he have been an angel? Eventually Vincent told his story to Jim Bramlett, an author who researches prophecies, and Jim used Vincent's experience, among others, in a magazine article.

Three years later, on Saturday, April 6th, 1996, Vincent awoke at 4:30 in the morning with a strong belief that he was to pray. He wasn't exactly sure about what, but this urge had come upon him before, and he had always obeyed it. He prayed for a few moments, then fell asleep.

At 7:00, Vincent awakened again and began his usual morning prayer time. About a half hour later, his telephone rang. It was too early to answer the phone on a Saturday, he decided, and continued praying. The answering machine would handle the call.

But the phone kept ringing. Insistently. Had Vincent forgotten to turn on the answering machine? No, he could see the red light from where he knelt. Vincent got up and went to the phone. Ten rings, eleven...and although the caller ID was also turned on, no number was showing. Vincent gave in and picked up the phone.

"Hello?"

"Hello" It was a woman's voice.

"Hello!" Vincent repeated.

"Hello!" the woman answered again.

"Yes--- did you want to speak to me?" Vincent was getting exasperated.

"No"

"Then why did you call?"

"I didn't call," the woman answered, as annoyed as he. *"You called me!"*

Vincent explained that he hadn't, that he had simply answered the phone. The very same thing had happened to the woman, whose name, she informed him, was Doris. *"I live in Iowa,"* she said. *"I can't imagine how this whole thing happened, Mr....?"*

"My name is Vincent Tan," he answered politely, planning to say goodbye and end this strange mix-up. But the woman gave a little gasp.

"Are you the Vincent Tan who had an experience with an angel?"

"Well, yes."

"My mother and I read about it in a magazine. We never forgot, what a wonderful story it was. Six months ago, my mother was diagnosed with terminal cancer. Every day since then, she has prayed that she might be able to speak with you before she died. This morning, I awakened at 3:30 and prayed, reminding the Lord of my mother's request."

Three thirty. Given the difference in time zones, Doris had awakened at the same moment as Vincent. They had been praying together.

"I can't believe this is happening," Doris went on. *"Would it be too much to ask you to talk to my mother?"*

"Put her on the phone," Vincent said.

The elderly lady's voice was weak and hardly audible, but for the next forty-five minutes or so, the two talked. Vincent told her about his angel experience in great detail, and they discovered that several of their favorite Scripture passages were the same. Finally, the elderly woman whispered, *"Praise the Lord, Amen."*

All became quiet. Thinking the old woman had fallen asleep, Vincent was about to hang up when Doris came back on the phone. *"Mother has died,"* she told Vincent. *"Thank you for what you did for her."*

Vincent was overwhelmed. A soul had just entered eternity, and he had been permitted to play a part in this joyous journey! He and Doris said their good-byes quickly, so she could begin the necessary arrangements. It was not until several hours later that he realized he had never gotten Doris's last name or address, nor had the caller ID recorded her number. And Vincent never received a bill for the call, although Doris had told him she had answered his ring.

Vincent saw no point in investigating further, for the experience, he believes, was simply part of God's plan. *"The Lord has his reasons for all of this,"* he says, *"And as we near the final hours, I know that He is even closer."*

Dan's notation:

This story is further proof that *Time is Short*. It has been given to us by God. This book contains one prophecy given by The Holy Spirit, and two more given by His angels, in which all are told that Jesus will be returning soon. These prophecies have been made known to me over the past four years, so this book could make them known to you. How many more people have received similar messages? In the United States? In the world? I am certain there are many more, just as I am convinced that God is certainly giving us notice to prepare.

Time is Short, and the form of this world is passing way. Behold, He is coming quickly!

> *Then I saw a new heaven and a new earth, for the first heaven and the first earth had passed away, and there was no longer any sea.*
> ***Revelation 21:1***

THE BEGINNING

Recommended Reading

Anderson, J. W., (2005), *The Power of Miracles: True stories of God's presence*, Loyola Press.

Blitz, M., (2014), *Blood Moons: Decoding the imminent heavenly signs*, WND Books.

Cahn, J., (2012), *The Harbinger: The ancient mystery that holds the secret of America's future*, Charisma House.

Coulter, J., and Coulter, S., (2016), *Until Death Do You Part: A story of faith, hope and love*,

Lester, K. I., (2013), *My Heavenly Encounter with Mom*, WestBow Press.

Neal, M. C., (2011), *To Heaven and Back: The true story of a doctor's extraordinary walk with God*, Circle 6 Publishing.

Strand, R., (1997), *Mini Moments with Angels*, New Leaf Publishing.

Online Reading:

I found a great website devoted to the gaining of spiritual gifts, Christian Prophecy.Org.UK. I believe you will find it useful. It is the reason why we should do these things.

GLOSSARY

Antichrist - Known as the 'Beast or 'the man of sin.' He will appear in the last days to declare himself God and persecute Christians in the great tribulation.

Backsliding - A Christian term referring to the returning to old sinful patterns of behavior.

Baptism - Christians are baptized in water to symbolize that we are dead and buried to our old way of life, and 'born again' in Christ.

Born Again - When we ask Jesus Christ into our lives as Lord and Savior, the experience can be so personally transformative, it can be said one has become a new person afterwards.

Demon or **Fallen Angels** - Angels who rebelled with Satan against God.

Elect or **Predestined** - Christians are called "The Elect." The term "Elect" refers to the fact that God chose (or "elected") us to be His children before He even created the world.

Evangelist - A person who seeks to inform others about the Christian faith.

Faith - Believing in God and in Him alone, in all He has done, and in His promises.

Gospel - The Good News! The good news that Jesus Christ, God the Son, became a sinless man. He died on the cross to pay the penalty for our sins. He rose from the dead, ascended into heaven, and will return to judge the living and the dead.

Holy Spirit - God is three persons in one: God the Father, the Son (Jesus) and the Holy Spirit. (Sometimes called The Holy Ghost.) The three in one form the Trinity.

Laying on of hands - Physically touching a person while praying for him or her for healing or to receive the holy spirit.

Men's Retreat - An event in which a group of men remove themselves from their normal routines to devote time to prayer and study.

Mercy - The act of being shown forgiveness in place of the punishment we would otherwise deserve.

Miracle - A supernatural act of God, something only God can do.

Nondenominational - Non-sectarian and open and accessible to any Christian. Not part of any Baptist, Methodist, Catholic, etc. denominations.

Prophet - A person given the gift of knowledge from God of present, future, or past events, to be used as God directs.

Saved - Rescued from the deserved punishment of sin (hell) by Jesus, and given instead grace and mercy (heaven) through believing in Jesus.

Dan Cassidy is available for book interviews and personal appearances. For more information contact:

Dan Cassidy
C/O Advantage Books
P.O. Box 160847
Altamonte Springs, FL 32716
info@advbooks.com

To purchase additional copies of this book visit our bookstore website at:
www.advbookstore.com

Longwood, Florida, USA
"we bring dreams to life" ™
www.advbookstore.com

www.ingramcontent.com/pod-product-compliance
Lightning Source LLC
Chambersburg PA
CBHW020911090426
42736CB00008B/584